CORPORATE
PLAYERS

CORPORATE PLAYERS

Designs for Working and Winning Together

ROBERT W. KEIDEL

WILEY

John Wiley & Sons

NEW YORK • CHICHESTER • BRISBANE • TORONTO • SINGAPORE

The author gratefully acknowledges permission to quote material from the following sources.

Automatic Data Processing, Inc., 1 ADP Boulevard, Roseland, NJ 07068

Melissa Mead and Jane Linder, Frito-Lay, Inc.: *A Strategic Transition* (A), case 9-187-065. Boston: Harvard Business School, 1986. Reprinted by permission.

Gareth Morgan, *Images of Organization.* Copyright © 1986 by Sage Publications. Reprinted by permission of Sage Publications, Inc.

Library of Congress Cataloging in Publication Data:

Keidel, Robert W.
  Corporate Players: Designs for working and winning together /
  Robert W. Keidel.

    p.   cm.
  ISBN 0-471-63176-0
  1. Organizational change. 2. Organizational effectiveness.
3. Work groups. I. Title.
HD58.8.K45 1988
658.4'02—dc19   87-28563
ISBN 0-471-63176-0   CIP

Printed in the United States of America

10 9 8 7 6 5 4 3 2 1

To My Family

Contents

Contents

Preface

This book, like everything else I've written, is work in process. It's my unfinished inventory of knowledge and ideas at a particular point. No doubt by the time *Corporate Players* is published, I will have had new insights, and reservations, that I'd pay dearly to see reflected in the final manuscript. Such is the nature of writing—and learning.

My first book, *Game Plans: Sports Strategies for Business,* was published in 1985. It represented a pulling together of concepts that I had been thinking about for four years. *Corporate Players,* while entirely freestanding, represents a logical next step. This book is distinctive in several ways. First and foremost, *Corporate Players* is a book for corporate managers, not general readers. It is concerned less with novelty than with application; less with sports-as-metaphor than with practical management tools. And where *Game Plans* tended to pattern organizations chiefly in terms of a single form of teamwork, *Corporate Players* emphasizes the importance of blending diverse kinds of teamwork.

Corporate Players could not have been written without extensive grounding in actual business situations. In both long-term consulting engagements and relatively short seminars, I have been able to test and refine my ideas about organizational design and teamwork as well as to conceive new ideas. In all, my consulting and writing have enriched each other. *Corporate Players* is a product of this interaction.

Acknowledgments

I've been truly fortunate for the opportunity to study under and/or work with some of the best in the business. From each of several individuals I have taken something different, yet always compatible. Russell Ackoff taught me the power of idealized design to produce organizational visions otherwise unobtainable. From William Foote Whyte I learned the importance of being receptive to settings and surprise—to appreciate all that the client brings to a research/consulting relationship. Michael Maccoby helped me understand how critical it is that organizational change be rooted in principles of human development. And because of Malcolm Shaw, I came to comprehend subtleties of human interaction that formerly had escaped me.

My greatest debt is to Eric Trist, with whom I began to study and work in 1974. Eric not only is the author of sociotechnical systems theory and what many today call "the team concept;" most fundamentally, he is an integrator. More than anyone else I have ever known, Eric is able to connect things—issues, concerns, concepts, systems, solutions. He is a bridge-builder whose own career has spanned the worlds of psychoanalysis, group dynamics, organizational design, and socio-ecological development. Eric's influence on my thinking has been profound. He has also been a wonderful friend.

Several colleagues, at Wharton and elsewhere, have provided helpful comments on various drafts of this book. They include Vinnie Carroll, Mary Daniels, John Eldred, Frank Farrow, Tom Gilmore, John Good, George McDaniel, Ken McGeary, Greg Shea, Bill Sommerfield, Gerry Susman, Michael Umen, and Gerry Zeitz. I also want to thank Peter Livingston, my literary agent, who placed the book with Wiley; John Mahaney, my editor at Wiley, for his many contributions over the course of the last year; and Alan Cohen and Glenn Morrison, who constructively reviewed my first complete manuscript.

Among the many clients who have sharpened my thinking—either by critiquing parts of *Corporate Players* or by reacting in real time to its key concepts—are Phil Barry, Rich D'Amato, John Dorsey, Ron Estridge, John Flannery, Bob Gibbons, Karol Kocourek, Karl Kraske, Bill Lucey, George Manners, Keith Otto, Abe Raab, Bud Rowell, Charlie Schroeder, Bob Smith, Ben Thorp, Frank Vitetta, and Derek Wendelken.

In keeping with tradition, the last paragraph belongs to my family. My parents, Philip and Phyllis Keidel, have been a continuing source of encouragement. My brother Biff and brothers-in-law Bill Bierlin and Tom Zitrides all have contributed valuable perspectives. On the home front, my kids have been into this project for some time. Andy has shown me new applications of the Teamwork Triangle, including one to an individual sport—karate, his first love. And Carly has convinced me that this graphic device has coloring-book potential; every room in our house is now decorated. Finally, to my wife, Carole, whose support has never wavered: you not only helped make it happen, you made it worth happening.

Introduction

It was one of the brightest groups I'd ever consulted with. And certainly one of the most industrious: the average work-week was easily 70 hours. The 10 managers—from divisional vice-president through functional specialists—all had impressive track records in their technically demanding industry. So why was the division struggling?

My earliest evidence came midway through our first off-site meeting, as the politeness of individual differences became oppressive. One manager captured the atmosphere perfectly: "It's like we're rolling ping-pong balls above the table and bowling balls below it."

"Team-building"—human relations skills, open communications, cooperative problem-solving—seemed to be exactly what was needed. At best, the performance of the group had been equal to the sum of its individual members' contributions; at worst, it had been far less than this. And from what I had been told, the group was never in sync—a point that would be reinforced in short order.

After four days of intensive team-building, exactly half the managers felt that the process had been too slow, too drawn out, while the other half were convinced that things had been rushed—with the consequence that minority points of view were never sufficiently considered. Still, it was agreed that the team-building we had started should continue.

But the more I worked with this group, the more convinced I became that conventional team-building was simply not enough. The problems weren't just a matter of interpersonal competence—"I'm OK, you're OK, we're OK." Rather, they were built into the organizational design that this group was now trapped in. Unless this design was changed, all the team-building in the world would make precious little difference.

Certain organizational units were isolated from each other when they should have been in close contact. Other units fought over resources that were supposed to be shared. Still other units wasted time in endless negotiations with the rest of the division when they would have functioned best on their own. Problems like these required changes in organizational structure as well as in process. Decision systems, information systems, reward systems, and physical layout all had to be addressed.

The group came to understand the need for such changes. In fact, key members took the lead in reconfiguring the design of their division—and their management team—in ways that would have been unimaginable in the past. Changes were made, not in lieu of team-building, but in conjunction with it. The combined result of these initiatives was a far more profitable, *competitive* business. And divisional management believed, with good reason, that the value of their redesign experience would extend well into the future.

They had learned conceptual tools for assessing and restructuring teamwork that could be applied and reapplied as situations required. It is exactly these tools that *Corporate Players* presents.

The time is ripe. The last few years have brought us:

Team Xerox
Team Nabisco
Team Pontiac
Jiffy Lube's J-Team
Comsat's Satellite Communications Team
Digital's Team Computer
Santa Fe Southern Pacific's New Team
Citicorp's World Class Corporate Trust Team
Intel's Team of Teams

Unfortunately, despite ritual appeals to teamwork, too many companies—and divisions and departments—still do not perform as highly effective teams. How come? I believe that the problem is conceptual. Most corporate appreciations of "team" and "teamwork" have the following shortcomings:

- They fail to *differentiate both teams and patterns of teamwork*. A team is a team is a team. Teamwork is teamwork is teamwork.

- They fail to appreciate the *holistic character of teamwork*—a combination of "soft" human relations and "hard" organizational design.

- They fail to appreciate the *strategic importance of teamwork*—that corporate effectiveness may depend as much on the quality of teamwork throughout the company as on any other factor.

Corporate Players is a response to all of these shortcomings. It is precisely because team and teamwork have become clichés that the title of this book is *Corporate PLAYERS,* not *Corporate TEAMS* or *Corporate TEAMWORK*. I wanted the book to have a fresh chance—rather than get labeled, on the basis of its title alone, as but one more tired team work treatise.

What is a "corporate player?" It is an individual, a multibillion-dollar corporation, or any unit in between. Probably the most familiar use of the term is to describe a whole company as a competitor in some kind of market- or industry-based "game" or "league." Note the paradox here. In sports and elsewhere, teams are made up of players. But corporate players in the broadest sense are clearly made up of teams . . . of teams. So players contain teams, just as teams contain players. For our purposes, then, corporate player and corporate team can be regarded as interchangeable.

I believe that our work structures mirror our game structures. Every corporation, and every unit within it, requires a unique blend of individual autonomy as in baseball; global control as in football; and voluntary cooperation as in basketball. Of course, baseball, football, and basketball all are team games and therefore have many features in common. But the differences among these sports are undeniable. The contrasts are most vivid at the professional level since the severity of competition compels teams to discover and master the essential character of their game. In a nutshell, baseball requires *situational* teamwork; football, *scripted* teamwork; and basketball, *spontaneous* teamwork. The design of these three sports serves as an underlying empirical base for *Corporate Players*. But regardless of how inclined you are to use sports metaphors, this book will show you how to mix and match the three basic teamwork alternatives to fit your distinctive needs.

If we have learned anything about corporate "excellence," it is that this quality is never once-and-for-all. There is no automatic pilot to lock onto. In the business arena, reaching the top may be easier than remaining there—just as in sports. As statistics for the present decade demonstrate, it is easier for a baseball team to win the World Series—or a football team the Superbowl, or a basketball team the NBA title—than to repeat as champions. (As of this writing, no team in any of these sports had won back-to-back titles in the 1980s.) Business is scarcely different. Pointing to models of corporate excellence without bounding them in time may be hazardous—as many observers (including myself) discovered when People Express Airlines went away.

The premise underlying *Corporate Players* is that adaptability—the capacity to adjust continuously to changing conditions—is rooted in *team competence*. Those companies that are team-competent—and therefore, able to integrate and apply different models of teamwork as situations dictate—will enjoy a significant competitive advantage over those that are not. They will have a repertoire of responses that can match whatever variety the environment confronts them with. Should the need arise for increased consistency, the organization can take systematic measures to emphasize central control. More local responsiveness required? Increase individual/unit autonomy. More flexibility? Reinforce spontaneous cooperation. Team competence means the ability to design and redesign—and operate—the right blend. The corporate division that I cited at the beginning of this Introduction has successfully made each kind of move, for one or more of its units, at different times. In the process, its managers have developed new confidence in their ability to manage change.

One caveat, however. As a client of mine once pointed out, "It's not enough to know what 'game' to play and how to play it. I may know my main game is baseball, but if I don't have the players, I have no chance. Without the talent, you just can't win." I could not agree more. My response was—and is—that both talent and team competence are critical and, to a degree, complementary. As will become apparent, particular team designs require particular abilities in addition to general ones. Knowing your game priorities can help you identify talents that are essential.

Corporate Players is written for managers, and especially for teams of managers. What can you expect from reading this book? Minimally, it will provide you with a whole new way of looking at and thinking about teamwork in your firm. You will also gain a communication vehicle of unusual potential. And, hopefully, you will come to see the opportunity for continuous change in a clearer, more positive light than ever before.

Corporate Players provides a framework that you can use to chart systematic organizational change. But I should caution that my conceptualization of corporate teamwork is deceptively simple. What I will describe verbally and graphically in relatively few pages goes to the heart of organizational strategy, structure, and style. Using these concepts as a change methodology is a serious matter that may require help from a consultant who understands both organizational design and team-building.

Corporate Players is organized as follows. Chapter 1 offers an historical overview of teamwork—what the concept has meant in the past, and what it means today. Chapter 2 provides a theoretical perspective by showing how the worlds of organizational design and team-building, so long separate, need to be brought together.

Chapter 3 presents the "Teamwork Profile," a systematic framework for analyzing organizational strategy, structure, and style. This chapter is actually a reference document, with an abundance of examples to help you understand the meaning of each dimension of the Teamwork Profile. Chapter 4 shows you how to use this framework, and the companion "Teamwork Triangle," in diagnosing your own organization. Chapter 5 lays out guidelines for articulating mission and clarifies the overlap between mission and organizational design.

Chapters 6 and 7 present a two-phase design methodology. Chapter 6, whose focus is *conceptualization*, contrasts three fundamental change alternatives and provides examples of each. Chapter 7 is concerned with *commitment*; it emphasizes the roles that the senior management team must play for organizational (re)design to succeed.

The final chapter synthesizes and expands. Chapter 8 argues that team competence is a function of the organization's "teamwork language;" consequently, the key to high performance is developing and using a language that matches the complexity and change the corporation faces.

Chapter One

Teamwork: Then and Now

I s there a corporation alive today that does not view itself as a team? Probably not. But what really constitutes a team? And what does "teamwork" mean? Many centuries ago, the word "team" meant "a set of draught animals; two or more oxen, horses, dogs, or other animals harnessed to draw together" (Oxford English Dictionary). It was not until the 17th century that "team" came to denote a number of persons who work together. This revised definition presaged the Industrial Revolution, which began near the end of the 18th century.

TEAMWORK ACROSS THREE ERAS

In the preindustrial, or agricultural, era, only rudimentary teamwork was required. Individuals and families could—and often did—go it alone. This was an age of autonomy—of the independent farmer, the forester, the frontiersman, the artisan. That teamwork which did take place was *situational* or episodic, and usually informal. It was often prompted by nature. If, for example, a tornado were to level the barn, neighbors would come together to put up another one. For the most part, however, organized collaboration among large numbers of people was the exception, not the rule.

In business, even into the last quarter of the 18th century, the dominant form of organization was the craft-based enterprise. Here, artisans and their apprentices worked independently to produce custom products. There was no master scheduling, no division of labor into discrete tasks, no standardization. Each craftsman worked at his own pace to produce a whole product that was different, often in very personal ways, from the products of other craftsmen.

The industrial era, which gathered force as the 19th century matured, turned things upside down. No longer did discretion reside with the worker. Control replaced autonomy. The shift was both initiated by and symbolized by Eli Whitney, the inventor of the cotton gin, who contracted with the government (in 1798) to produce 10,000 complete stands of muskets within two years. Whitney set out to convert his factory into a high-volume production machine. In so doing, he redefined the nature of manufacturing: coordination became a matter of system-wide planning and monitoring.[1] Further refinements of mass production—which were brought about in turn by such now-well-known figures as Isaac Singer, Samuel Colt, and Henry Ford—culminated in the modern assembly line, a near-pure expression of the "machine theory of organization." Sociologist Daniel Bell observed in 1956: the "three logics of size, time, and hierarchy converge in that great achievement of industrial technology, the assembly line: the long . . . lines require huge shed space; the detailed breakdown of work imposes a set of mechanically paced and specified motions; the degree of coordination creates new technical, as well as social, hierarchies."[2]

What sort of teamwork did we find under these conditions? *Scripted* teamwork—teamwork meticulously choreographed at the top. Each worker had a narrow, precisely-defined part to play in a synoptic plan that he only dimly comprehended. The generic organizational type of this era was the centralized, functional bureaucracy—made up of departments representing each "function" (manufacturing, sales, finance, and so on)—and centrally coordinated. In every case, the boundaries of teamwork—when and where to interact, with whom, and usually how—were articulated from above. Such was also the case in those industrial-era organizations concerned not with mass-producing goods but with administering high-volume services and processing reams of paper.

The pattern of scripted teamwork remained as true for

organizational units as for individuals. This was especially apparent when bureaucracies vertically integrated—that is, acquired suppliers "upstream" and/or customers "downstream." The reason for vertical integration typically was (and is) control: to minimize the likelihood of glitches in the long-linked economic chain from the raw-material source to final consumer. "Teamwork" at a macro level, therefore, paralleled that at the micro level of the high-volume plant.

Scripted teamwork also characterized the successor to functional bureaucracy, the divisional firm—a design that had its origins in the 1920s and 1930s. As historian Alfred Chandler has shown, General Motors and a handful of other major companies (notably Du Pont, Sears Roebuck, and Standard Oil of New Jersey) adopted this new structure primarily to gain control over diversification run amok. What resulted was essentially a cloning of the original: the divisional firm became roughly the sum of many smaller bureaucracies—most of which continued to require scripted teamwork. Ironically, however, the divisionalized structure reintroduced autonomy—at least for the general managers of the smaller bureaucracies. These individuals tended to have considerable operating freedom vis-à-vis the corporate office (although they were apt to run their own shows with an iron hand).

The industrial era peaked about forty years ago. In fact just about thirty years ago, in the mid-1950s, we reached a point where, for the first time, the number of white-collar workers exceeded the number of blue-collar production workers. Most of the white-collar jobs involved information processing—by managers, professionals, technicians, and clerical workers. According to MIT professor David Birch, by 1984 only 10 percent of the American population was actually making things.[3] Thus it seems fitting that this postindustrial era be described as an "information" era.

· 4 ·

The postindustrial era is characterized by increasing change, complexity, and interdependence. We are witnessing an explosion in knowledge and technology that has already led to product life-cycles a fraction of what they were just a few years ago. No one has reason to believe that things will slow down. The postindustrial environment is, in a word, turbulent. Under such conditions, organizations have no choice but to experiment with new structures that can match ever-tougher competitive demands.

Perhaps the most prominent "postindustrial" organizational type is the matrix, which originated in the aerospace industry during the late 1950s and 1960s in response to simultaneous pressures for state-of-the-art technology on the one hand and cost/schedule performance on the other. From the late 1960s on, matrix organizations have been an oft-tried, if difficult, solution to the general problem of achieving a balance of two criteria: responsiveness (autonomy) and efficiency (control). Advocates of matrix seek the best of both these worlds.

In a matrix organization, certain managers have two bosses—for instance, one boss who is in charge of a product or market or customer, and another who is responsible for a resource department such as engineering or production or information services. The basic idea behind this design is to force "two-boss managers" to think like generalists; that is, to weigh different points of view (such as customer needs versus organizational capabilities) when making a decision.

Along with the matrix structure have come several usually temporary small-team varieties, such as task forces and project teams (the terms are interchangeable), which are made up of individuals from various parts and levels of the organization. These units typically take a multidisciplinary approach either to solving problems (e.g., a quality defect or a production snag) or to coordinating new developments (such as the manufacture of a new product line or the start-up of a new facility).

Common to both these designs—matrix and task force/project team—is an emphasis on a new kind of teamwork: *spontaneous*. Individuals and organizational units must willingly cooperate in a way that cuts across boundaries of hierarchy, location, division, department, and discipline. For the first time, discretionary teamwork—down, up, and across—is essential to corporate survival.

In the preindustrial era the need for teamwork was scant, and that teamwork which did occur was inchoate. The industrial era ushered in an entirely new concept: teamwork that resembled clockwork. System designers planned, managers controlled, and workers carried out marching orders. The changes postindustrial society requires are even more profound, especially for corporate managers. Not only must they learn and internalize a new form of teamwork; far more than their predecessors, postindustrial managers must be able to integrate and apply the diverse forms of teamwork—situational, scripted, and spontaneous. Preindustrial managers—such as there were—could leave well enough alone. Industrial managers could leave nothing alone. Postindustrial managers must know when to be hands-off, when to be hands-on, and when to work hand-in-hand.

Like scientific progress, the three eras have been both discontinuous and cumulative. Each new era has brought with it peculiar teamwork requirements but, at the same time, has had to be synthesized with the logic of past eras. In fact, the outlines of postindustrial organization were visible in preindustrial times: the craft organizations of the late 18th century relied on cooperation as well as individual initiative.[4] But whereas such organizations employed simple, stable techniques, their postindustrial counterparts have to master complex, dynamic technologies. The bottom line? Getting the right blend of corporate "teamwork" has never been more difficult than it is today—and never more important.

LEARNING FROM TEAM SPORTS

Fortunately, there is a realm of experience from which managers can learn: organized athletic competition. When you think about it, what better place is there to look for models of teamwork than professional team sports? Indeed, Barbara Tuchman has suggested that *"Homo ludens,* man at play, is surely as significant a figure as man at war or at work. In human activity, the invention of the ball may be said to rank with the invention of the wheel."[5]

The three major pro team sports in the United States— baseball, football, and basketball—provide structural models of the three generic forms of teamwork in business. Interestingly, the order in which these games appeared and became organized—like the games themselves—parallels the historical eras. Baseball's National League was established in 1876, its American League in 1900; the National Football League (NFL) was created in 1922; and the National Basketball Association (NBA) was formed in 1949. Baseball is essentially preindustrial; football, industrial; and basketball, postindustrial.

Baseball is a metaphor for the autonomy of organizational parts. The essence of this game is the pitcher–batter confrontation. Each player is pretty much on his own. Apart from setting up a pitching rotation and positioning fielders, the manager need not worry about coordination, as this is achieved through the design of the sport.

Teamwork in baseball is situational. It is dictated primarily by the batter's reactions to "nature," in the form of pitches thrown by the opposing pitcher. (Of the three sports, only in baseball does the defense always put the ball into play.) Granted, there are myriad instances of the manager's directing a batter to "take" (that is, not swing at) a pitch or to lay down a bunt, or directing a baserunner to try to steal a base. But such incremental ploys pale in significance compared to the effects of power hitting,[6] which cannot be choreographed.

Football is a metaphor for hierarchical control over organizational parts. Players' roles are tightly specified, and each play is a meticulously crafted protocol that guides every player in the game. Teamwork is scripted by the head coach. Only a few of the NFL's 28 teams allow the quarterback to call his own plays (with the exception of permitting him to "check off" at the line of scrimmage in response to a peculiarity that he notices in the defense's alignment). The logic for such prescribed teamwork is twofold: (1) the discontinuous nature of the game allows ample time for top-down planning, and (2) the coaching staff has a global view both of the field (aided as they are by spotters high in the pressbox) and of the contest (by having the opportunity to think several plays ahead without having to worry about being squashed by 300-pound behemoths).

Basketball is a metaphor for voluntary cooperation among organizational parts—for spontaneous teamwork. At the professional level, teamwork in basketball is dictated in large part by the players themselves. Because the game is more continuous than football, the basketball coach is in less of a position than his football counterpart to script each play. On the other hand, cooperation in basketball, unlike that in baseball, is not defined by the natural evolution of a play. Rather, cooperation is discretionary. Players repeatedly face situations in which they must elect whether or not to cooperate.

Some, of course, might object that these three sports are

too "American" to serve as models for world-class business. With football, such individuals may have a point. "American" football is idiosyncratic to the United States—perhaps a reflection of the fact that this nation has taken the concept of mass production farther than has any other part of the globe.[7] Both football and mass production exhibit an asymmetry—between coaches and players, planners and doers, managers and workers—that is largely absent from the other games, and from other forms of work organization.

Baseball, unlike football, is played throughout the Americas and across the Orient. And basketball is by any measure international; it may now be played in more countries than even soccer.[8]

As models of organizational design and teamwork, basketball and soccer are actually quite close: Both games place a premium on self-management and flexibility. Both are androgynous (that is, they are played by men and women), readily understandable, and intimate in the sense that each depends on the ability and resolve of players to work together spontaneously. Coincidentally, the first ball ever used in basketball—by the game's inventor, James Naismith—was a soccer ball.

It is also fair to include volleyball in the same category as basketball and soccer—and not just because the ball is so similar. Although volleyball is less continuous than basketball or soccer, the game has a compensating feature that basketball and soccer lack: every player rotates through every position.

The *international* style of ice hockey also has much in common with basketball. Unlike the *dump-and-chase* style—hockey's equivalent to grind-it-out football—the international game stresses transition (rather than possession), generalist skills, and spontaneous teamwork. It is a game of finesse, not intimidation—of passing, not pummeling.[9]

FAMILIAR EXPERIENCES
WITH TEAMWORK

For those in or about to enter business who never played team sports as kids, the very concept of teamwork must cause confusion. What models can one then identify with? If my own personal experience is at all representative, the non-sports models of teamwork that come our way are biased and conflicting. The problem starts with the barely bridled individualism of our educational system, where "teamwork" means little more than allowing others their turn to speak up in the classroom. From first grade on, so many of us are each charged with the monumental importance of getting not just "A's" but "all A's." Pulling this off means outperforming others. So it's the individual student versus the rest of the class.

The pressure heats up as the grade levels go up. Nowhere is this more apparent than in graduate business schools, where the Master of Business Administration (MBA) degree has become the most popular graduate credential in the nation. (Between 1950 and 1986, nearly one million students earned MBA degrees; in fact in 1986 alone, 71,000 new MBAs were minted.[10]) How to win a high starting salary? Get top grades. How to get top grades? Excel individually. Sure, there is some group work—jointly preparing cases, sharing responsibility for making a seminar lively. But what really counts is soloing. It is hardly surprising, then, that the best and brightest who enter our major corporations are often more comfortable competing against, rather than cooperating with, other individuals. How else could they have thrived in an educational system that is preindustrial in its emphasis on individual autonomy?

Once in a corporation, however, the new MBA—or other business recruit—is likely to discover a very different form of teamwork. He or she is apt to find the individualism of formal education replaced by a bureaucratic, perhaps even military, model in which "teamwork" means compliance. What is now important is to become known as a "team player"—often a euphemism for one who readily suppresses his or her own goals for the sake of the larger organization. The individual's power to do his or her own thing is replaced by hierarchical power over, and submission to, others. That is, preindustrial autonomy is replaced by industrial-strength control.

At least, this was my experience—from business school in the mid-1960s to a large corporation in the early 1970s. Are things all that different now for the typical MBA? I doubt it. Investment bankers and entrepreneurs notwithstanding, my guess is that the autonomy-to-control kind of culture jolt is still a common pattern for many of those going from college to corporation. For despite the Steve Jobses, Ross Perots, and even Jack Welches of today's world, the conformist "organization man" popularized by William H. Whyte over thirty years ago is still very much with us. Whyte himself has recently claimed that "The United States continues to be dominated by large organizations, and they are run much as they were before. The people who staff them are pretty much the same as those who did before. . . . For all the talk of a new breed of managers, what most companies seem to want is this [uniform corporate] profile as it was before."[11]

Outside of sports, I never fully experienced the third teamwork model—voluntary cooperation—until I began carrying out action research with Eric Trist, in the mid-1970s, as part of a Wharton doctoral program in social systems sciences. Collaborative work with clients was a cornerstone of this curriculum.

Most managers probably encounter the voluntary cooperation model only (if ever) after investing several years in one or more corporations. The model usually appears under the banner "team-building" and has to do with the *process* of human interaction: disclosing feelings, giving and receiving feedback, learning how to solve problems consensually.

Some managers embrace team-building principles and are able to incorporate them successfully in their management style. But too many others become confused or cynical about the concept. For more often than not, the collegiality and openness espoused in team-building bump up against the tough *power* realities of corporate life. An either/or struggle ensues, the outcome of which is predictable: *power beats process*. It's just as Woody Allen once put it: "The lion and the lamb may lie down together, but the lamb won't get much sleep."

Given this sequence—from educational autonomy to corporate control to cooperation-in-the-face-of-control—is it any wonder that so many managers wind up with limited or conflicting notions of teamwork? In the past, this state of affairs could be endured. The world was sufficiently slow-moving, and competition sufficiently local and restrained, that team incompetence was affordable. No more.

David Birch has asserted that "For every corporation in the U.S., the best predictor of death is stability."[12] Increasing organizational flux—through technological change, growth, retrenchment, diversification, acquisition, divestiture, leveraged buyout, and merger—means that the demands on managers to lead many and different teams will only grow more severe. Currently, one-half to two-thirds of all mergers and acquisitions fail. Much of the blame has been placed (properly) on inept people-management, that is, on ineffective organizational design and teamwork. In the future, managers who succeed will be those who, above all else, are team-competent.

TEAM COMPETENCE

Team competence requires redefining the manager's role. Increasingly, the key tasks are facilitating and enabling rather than directing and controlling. Managers must become adept at helping groups learn how to coordinate themselves. The operative phrases are paradoxical: stimulating spontaneous teamwork; managing voluntary cooperation.

Voluntary cooperation is no less important *among* organizations. Just look at the number of corporate joint ventures now taking place. Or consider the mounting pressures brought to bear by stakeholders other than stockholders— such as regulatory agencies, consumer groups, environmentalists, unions/employee associations, and the communities in which firms reside. "Win-win" dynamics with each of these external constituencies are clearly in the corporation's long-term interests.

But while both managers and their corporations must increasingly display voluntary cooperation on many fronts, organizational requirements for individual/unit freedom and global perspective will persist. The challenge for all corporate players is to increase cooperative capacities and at the same time, integrate this behavior with appropriate responses to legitimate organizational needs for autonomy and control. Metaphorically, although the general requirement is to play more basketball, every particular situation will require a unique blend that includes baseball and football.

In organizations throughout our society, the relative importance of control is declining, but some measure of control will always remain necessary. For its part, autonomy appears to be on the upswing—what with recent trends such as deregulation, privatization, corporate decentralization, and entrepreneurship. Figure 1.1 contrasts the organizational/teamwork demands of the postindustrial era with those of past eras.

Figure 1.1. Relative Importance of Autonomy, Control, and Cooperation—by Era

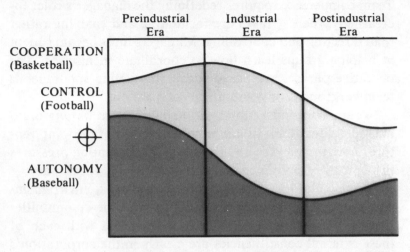

Postindustrial managers face a more daunting future than their predecessors did. But this future is also a more stimulating one—one with unbounded opportunities for learning and development. A good thing—because organizational innovations will be required that rival technological advances. It will no longer be possible—if indeed it still is—to succeed while believing naively that a team is a team is a team.

Mainstream concepts of teamwork have failed to keep pace with the competitive realities confronting most corporations. Chapter 2 lays out the shortcomings of current teamwork theory and practice and shows why it is essential to integrate the "hard" teamwork implicit in organizational design with the "soft" teamwork explicit in team-building.

Chapter Two

The Two Worlds
of Corporate Teamwork

Organizational design has to do with structures and systems: how coordination is achieved, where decision-making authority resides, how information and rewards are allocated, what physical configuration is used. Team-building is concerned with small-group dynamics—how well people get along with one another, how much they trust and respect each other, how effectively they work together.

Ask any "hardball" organizational design consultant about team-building and the reply is likely to be "It's touchy-feely fluff—all milk and honey." Conversely, ask a "softball" team-builder what organizational design means and you will probably be told, "It's just a bunch of boxes—a matter of rearranging boxes." Two different worlds if ever there were. The separation between these worlds remains one of the largest barriers to corporate team competence.[1]

How does your corporation or unit pursue teamwork? Chances are it is in one of two ways: implicitly, through organizational design; or explicitly, through a process of team-building. Although many companies can legitimately claim that they "do" both, it is the rare firm that consciously puts these two pieces together. Yet this synthesis is what every organization must accomplish if it is to realize its full potential.

Let's take organizational design and team-building in turn. What does each entail, and in what ways is each only a partial response to developing team competence?

IMPLICIT TEAMWORK THROUGH ORGANIZATIONAL DESIGN

The idea here is that by getting structures and systems right, the necessary teamwork will happen automatically. At its simplest, organizational design is one-dimensional. It is a continuum between centralization and decentralization—a rail along which the organization, a trolley, travels back and forth. For Robert E. Levinson, former president of Steelcraft Manufacturing and author of *The Decentralized Company,* organizational design is a Star Wars-like struggle between the forces of evil ("centralized management") and the forces of good ("radical decentralization").[2] Edmund T. Pratt, Jr., CEO of Pfizer, Inc., views the matter more dispassionately but in similar terms; for him, organizational design boils down to companies "passing each other going towards centralization or decentralization."[3]

The problem with one-dimensional organizational design is its "either/or" nature. Teamwork is narrowly construed either as a major concern of the top (and, therefore, to be built into the organization's structure by the top) or as a minor concern of the bottom (and not worth worrying about). At best, one-dimensional conceptualizations verge on two dimensions. They try to realize aspects of both centralization and decentralization. In the spirit of blending, *Vanguard Management* author James O'Toole claims that "Since the early part of this century, the primary problem of big-company management has been to find ways to simultaneously obtain the benefits of centralization *and* decentralization."[4]

Decentralization and centralization—or more generally, autonomy (freedom) and control (order)—constitute the core managerial vocabulary on organizational design.[5] Consultant Stanley Davis puts the matter as follows: "all forms of organization have two simultaneous needs that are often at odds with each other: freedom and order. . . . Freedom is translated as the specialized interests of different parts, the optimal goal of decentralization. Order is represented as the regulation and integration of all those parts in harmonious and common action, the optimal goal of centralization."[6]

What's wrong with this portrayal? It stresses only two-thirds of the picture. The third "need" that all organizations have is for *cooperation*—specifically, *voluntary cooperation*.

The R&D vice president of a fast-growing high-tech company once hurled the following charge at me, only half in jest: "You business-school people are incapable of thinking in more than two dimensions." After stumbling through a denial, I began to give his observation some real thought. I concluded that my client, a Ph.D. chemist, was more on target than off. Where indeed would business schools (not to mention consulting firms) be without two-dimensional matrices? Whether it be a growth/share 2x2, a product/mission 3x3, or a 9x9 "managerial grid," the simple matrix is hard to resist. No wonder so many of us in or around business schools have an almost knee-jerk tendency to force problems into two-dimensional screens.

Of course, there is good reason for this tendency; the use of two-dimensional schemes has its positive side. Graphically, it's difficult to express more than two dimensions on paper. And to be sure, most complex organizational problems can be framed in terms of the interaction of a small number of "strategic" variables—sometimes as small a number as two. Thus, it is not surprising that organizational design continues to be treated as a two-dimensional issue in so many corporations. But two-dimensional thinking limits the options. Here are some examples that show why:

CASE ONE. A major corporation analyzed its decision system and then specified what it wanted the system to look like in the future. Every business function—R&D, production, sales and marketing, personnel, finance, and so on—and every operating unit was taken into account. Each decision area was characterized as "corporate" (that is, to be handled at headquarters), "local" (at operating locations), or a combination of these patterns.

What this vocabulary failed to consider were those decisions that should be *shared* between operating units (chiefly, divisions and facilities) and indeed, between functions. The approach to decision-making was limited to mandating (centralization) and delegating (decentralization); it ignored collaborating (sharing). Hence, opportunities for synergy across the corporation—through lateral interaction—were not highlighted. A postscript: subsequent efforts have recognized this gap and are focused on identifying and exploiting synergies throughout the company; these efforts are proving highly fruitful.

CASE TWO. At a manufacturing plant, three machining centers were in need of new material-handling equipment. While not identical, these centers had essentially similar material-handling requirements. The traditional alternatives for the operations manager were simple: unilaterally decide what equipment to buy (mandate) or leave the decision up to each machining center supervisor (delegate).

The problem with mandating was twofold: (1) it assumed that the manager was sufficiently knowledgeable to make the best decision, and (2) it excluded his subordinates from a decision that directly affected them—a blow to their morale. Delegating also had its drawbacks. If the manager were to allow each of the three people reporting to him to do his or her own thing, a lot of fact-finding would be duplicated. And since each individual was likely to want a different process, purchasing-scale discounts would be lost. Moreover, different processes would mean more complicated maintenance and no interchangeability of repair parts, thus increasing inventory.

The third option—and the one chosen—was to bring together the three machining center supervisors to mutually hash out the pros and cons of different options—and then agree on one that best met everybody's needs. This decision process, which tapped everyone's knowledge and interest, was effective and efficient—and empowering. It recognized the technical knowledge of the three supervisors and therefore reinforced their sense of professionalism; it also provided these individuals with an important peer-support experience.

CASE THREE. A firm that has grown rapidly, in large part by acquiring other companies, has resolved to develop technical capabilities second to none in its industry. At present, technical units (product and process R&D) are a patchwork of centralization and decentralization—the legacy of a long string of acquisitions.

The respective strengths of centralization and decentralization are well understood by the corporation, and the technical structure of the future will no doubt incorporate a systematic mix of these approaches. But the new arrangement may also feature something different: "distributed technical expertise."

The company is now looking for ways to identify nodes of technical excellence wherever they exist in the system. Such capabilities would then become available to all other parts of the corporation on an as-requested basis. This arrangement has distinct advantages over centralized and decentralized alternatives. On one hand, it avoids the political barriers that go up whenever precious skills become lodged in a centralized corporate staff function; hence, the new arrangement should be user-friendly. On the other hand, it makes special capabilities available to all in the organization—and not the exclusive property of the unit in which they happen to reside; as a result, it leverages these competencies.

In each of these cases, the options are not just a mix of A and B. Rather, the options encompass A, B, and C. Organizational design is always a blend of A, B, and C. That said, however, it is important to point out the danger of attempting to realize A, B, and C in equal measure. Such, I believe, is the fundamental flaw in matrix organization.

As Chapter 1 indicated, matrix is a postindustrial design that tries to achieve the best of two worlds: autonomy and control.[7] A conventional critique of matrix is that it muddles priorities. By trying to jointly optimize two dimensions, this design runs the risk of optimizing neither. The real problem with matrix, however, is that it unknowingly attempts to jointly optimize not two but *three* dimensions: autonomy, control, *and cooperation*. This is an extremely tough act to pull off, especially for very long. Texas Instruments is famous for its claim that "more than two objectives is no objectives." The same logic applies to organizational design priorities: more than two primary dimensions is no primary dimensions. Hence, matrix organization seems to be an inherently unstable design.[8]

To sum up: relying on one- or two-dimensional organizational design to produce superior teamwork is loading the dice against yourself. The implicit teamwork that to some extent flows from organizational design must be complemented with explicit teamwork—through team-building.

EXPLICIT TEAMWORK
THROUGH TEAM-BUILDING

Team-building has to do with human relations and patterns of interaction. Whereas organizational design may cover large groups—even hundreds of thousands of people—team-building necessarily involves groups that are small enough for everyone to interact face-to-face. A team-building menu typically includes:

- *Team definition.* Who belongs on the team? Who are the primary players, supporting players, and peripheral players?

- *Role clarification.* Who is responsible for what tasks? Who must interact with whom in order to accomplish his/her tasks?

- *Goal acceptance.* To what extent do people understand and buy into team goals?

- *Work climate.* How open, trusting, and stimulating is the workplace environment?

- *Communication style/feedback.* How authentically and effectively do team members communicate with each other? Which behavioral patterns should be reinforced, which discontinued, and which changed?

- *Problem-solving/action-planning.* What practical next steps should the team take in order to improve both its process and its performance?

- *Interteam relations.* How can conflict be reduced, and trust increased, between teams that must cooperate with each other in order to achieve their missions?

For the most part, conventional team-building concentrates on "soft" areas that collectively define a team's style. Rarely will this process venture very far into such "hard" concerns as business strategy, organizational structure, and systems—decision systems, information systems, reward systems, and the like. Team-building's bias for the soft is understandable given the implicit concept of a team that it represents. Perhaps the most basic assumption is that team members need to interact frequently and over extended periods of time. A related assumption is that members provide complementary skills—that they each make partial but mutual contributions. Together, interaction and complementarity are assumed to yield positive synergy, a state in which team performance significantly exceeds the sum of individual contributions.

The concept of teamwork inherent in team-building is narrow. Team members are expected to cooperate spontaneously—that is, without waiting for direction from a manager or supervisor. In fact, often implicit (and sometimes explicit) in team-building is the notion that an effective team does not need a guiding leader at all but rather, can function as an autonomous entity.

With team-building's bias for voluntary intimacy, it is understandable that certain organizational units may question whether the process is relevant to them. Consider the following initial reactions during the first day of scheduled team-building sessions that I recently led:

- What are we doing here? We're obviously not a team. In fact, we hardly ever see each other.

  Salesperson, meeting with a group of peers from several geographical regions

- We're not like a business team. They have to work together as a unit, but we don't. We were selected for this work just because we're soloists.

  Research scientist, meeting with others from the top three levels of a product-design department

- From what I've heard, team-building is a joke. All loosey-goosey. Our operation's got to run tight. You start screwing around with it and it would be a disaster.

  Machine operator, meeting with the rest of his extended machine crew

All of these complaints are perfectly legitimate. They reflect team-building's major omission—attention to the hard aspects of organizational design. To be effective, team-building needs to take into account design issues of decentralization and centralization, just as organizational design should incorporate the soft dimension of sharing.

ROOT DIFFERENCES BETWEEN ORGANIZATIONAL DESIGN AND TEAM-BUILDING

Organizational design—at least in the West—has been a vertical concept, while team-building and its implied model of teamwork have been conceived as horizontal or lateral. George Lakoff and Mark Johnson, in a stimulating book titled *Metaphors We Live By*,[9] show how deeply the vertical metaphor is ingrained in our western culture. Good is up, bad is down. High status is up, low status is down. High-tech, low tech; upscale, downscale; high road, low road; high-life, low-life, and so on. One need not look very far to appreciate the pervasiveness of the vertical metaphor in organizational thinking. Thus we have high-level and low-level jobs along the corporate ladder, top-down versus bottom-up planning and change, up in the office versus down on the factory floor. The hourly worker is clearly one down; the top manager is just as clearly one up—especially if he is tall. A recent study of MBA graduates that correlated height and earnings determined that each extra inch is worth about $600 per year.[10]

Comic George Carlin has captured the difference in terms of team sports language. In baseball, the question is "Who's *up*?" In football, it's "What *down* is it?" The structural parallels with corporations run deep. Baseball exemplifies decentralization, football centralization. In baseball, each player is essentially an autonomous decision-maker—so that in effect, the flow is bottom-up. In football, decision-making is chiefly the province of the head coach and his staff—and his surrogate on the field, the quarterback; the flow is top-down. These differences are vividly mirrored by the physical location of the manager (baseball) and head coach (football) in relation to their players. In baseball, the manager is literally below ground level, in the dugout; he must look up to witness his players and the game. In football, the head coach is standing while his players are hunched over; in fact, the top-down character of this relation is best symbolized by the spotter high in the pressbox, who feeds overviews of the game to the coaching staff standing on the sidelines, who send in plays to the crouching quarterback, who directs the actions of "down linemen," so-called because their hands are on the ground. In baseball it is the player who is "up"; in football it is the coach. Baseball and football are simply contrasting models of vertical organizational design.

Basketball exemplifies mutuality. The game is essentially horizontal—no small irony, given the height of the players. (The average player in the NBA stands 6'8".) In fact, one of the greatest big men of all time, former Boston Celtic center Bill Russell, has observed that "in competitive basketball most of the critical distances are horizontal, along the floor or at eye level. Height is not as important as it may seem, even in rebounding."[11] Russell goes on to note that fully three-quarters of all rebounds are taken at or below the level of the basket's rim. The lateral quality of the game is also demonstrated by the physical relation of the coach to his team. The basketball coach is courtside, routinely communicating with his players while play is in progress—and even in a position to pat a player on the back while the game goes on.

Traditional organizational design—dominated by decentralization (as in baseball) and centralization (as in football)—is atomistic: the organization can very nearly be decomposed into its constituent parts or processes. In decentralized organizations, the performance of the whole is approximated by the sum of the actions of its product/market (output) units. The most familiar example of this type is the conglomerate or holding company, whose operating divisions have almost nothing to do with each other or with corporate headquarters.

In centralized organizations, overall performance is—at least in theory—essentially the cumulative sum of the actions of its functional (input) units. The prototype of centralization is the old-line, single-product firm where interactions among functions—R&D ("design it"), manufacturing ("make it"), and marketing ("sell it")—are sequential, minimal, and predictable, and are orchestrated primarily by senior management.

There is less modularity in basketball-like organizations than in either centralized or (especially) decentralized organizations. In basketball analogues, as in the process of team-building, the parts and their contributions are hard to separate. Actions count for far less than interactions. Again, it's the difference between football/baseball and basketball. Football and baseball are both discontinuous games in which most of the players have fixed positions and are relatively stationary in anticipation of the next play. By contrast, basketball is continuous, with all positions flexible and fluid. In a fundamental sense, the game is circular.

Team-building processes are also circular. This quality is reinforced by some of the language used. Cooperative problem-solving methodologies typically "cycle" and "recycle" through a circular set of stages. And indeed, we have quality *circles*, not rectangles. The term parallels (if not follows) the Japanese tendency, noted by Richard Pascale and Anthony Athos, to carry out dialogue in circles, expanding or contracting as sensibilities dictate. As Pascale and Athos further explain, "a Japanese does not see his world in terms of separate categories (friends, relatives, subordinates), but as concentric rings of relationships, from the intimate (at the innermost) to the peripheral."[12] Clearly, team-building is a round-table activity—even if round tables are hard to come by in many corporate conference rooms.

The reciprocal, circular, interactive processes that characterize team-building may help to explain why the third design dimension that it represents—voluntary cooperation—is so often ignored as an explicit design criterion. These processes are ethereal. You can't pin them down. Out of sight, very possibly out of mind. But low visibility renders circular processes no less important. Boston Celtic legend Red Auerbach put the matter poignantly in basketball terms: "The chemistry is more important than a man. *You get enough intangibles, they become a tangible and put points on the board.*"[13]

To understand the flow of a basketball game, you have to comprehend overall patterns. A basketball game cannot be reduced to the actions of individuals or even clusters (platoons) of individuals. Players are constantly in motion except when someone is shooting free throws—the only modular aspect of the game. In abstract terms, the more spontaneous interaction among a team's—an organization's—parts, the less readily one can isolate individual/departmental contributions.

Here, I believe, is the underlying reason that organizational designers have difficulty with team-building concepts. They find it tough to "assemble" structures that (1) they cannot easily visualize and (2) they cannot neatly decompose into parts and recompose out of parts. Alternatively, team-builders often seem instinctively to resist that which is analytical. It is as if any effort to be hard, concrete, or structural is "bad" because it robs human interaction of some wonderful mystery.

Both approaches are wrong. Each perspective needs the other. Only when organizational design and team-building are joined will organizational performance approach its potential.

INTEGRATING ORGANIZATIONAL DESIGN AND TEAM-BUILDING

Integrating organizational design and team-building—hard and soft—dissolves the long-standing feud between those who claim that different situations call for different styles of leadership and management, and others who argue that there is one best way to lead and manage—participatively. They're both right (and wrong). A participative approach can be effective under most circumstances; it simply cannot be taken as far in some instances as in others. The earlier quote by a machine operator ("Our operation's got to run tight") is a case in point. In many highly structured contexts, such as closely-sequenced machining centers, participation just can't have free rein. You cannot run most factories (or indeed, companies) on spontaneity. Yet some participation is almost always possible—and useful.

So it's a matter of both/and, not either/or. With respect to teamwork, it's a matter of nature as well as degree. Incredible though it may seem, most team-builders still fail to differentiate both "teamwork" and "teams." They—and therefore, the managers they advise—persist with a binary view. A group or unit is either a team or a non-team. The implication is that all teams must have essentially the same properties; in effect, that they must resemble a basketball team.

After more than two years of team-building with a variety of business units at one client site, I was approached by the materials manager, who wanted to try a similar process with his department. After our first few sessions, this individual was distraught. He could not understand how his staff—who were accustomed to working independently of him and of each other—could possibly constitute a team. He even wrote an open letter to his department titled, "Are we a team?" It was only after this manager and his staff had analyzed their department from an organizational design perspective that they understood the real issue. The relevant question was not "*Are* we a team?" but rather, "*What kind* of team are we?" All agreed that they were a highly decentralized team of soloists who needed to work together only on a limited basis. When members did need to interact, a "basketball" pattern was helpful. But the department remained—appropriately— a baseball team.

In fact, the issue of management style—one-best-way versus situational—is a variation on a larger issue: universal principles of management versus contingency theory. Advocates of contingency theory claim that, as Jay Galbraith has put it, although there is no one best way to organize, not all ways of organizing are equally effective.[14] Effectiveness depends on getting the best organizational match with external conditions. Those who espouse universal principles, such as Tom Peters and Bob Waterman—first together, and now separately—argue that in all situations certain precepts are critical. As with style, both camps are right.

THREE ORGANIZATIONAL DESIGNS

Different theorists and consultants use different graphic devices and different vocabularies to elaborate key aspects of organizational design. Harold Leavitt constructed a *diamond* made up of task, structure, people, and technology.[15] McKinsey & Co. portrays its "7-S framework"® as an *atom* to depict what it considers to be the seven major, interdependent organizational variables: strategy, structure, systems, skills, staff, style, and shared values.[16] Jay Galbraith has chosen a five-pointed *star*—made up of task, structure, information and decision processes, reward systems, and people—to summarize his concept of the key, interdependent organization design variables.[17]

I'm partial to *triangles*—and triads. I believe that many (if not most) multi-dimensional organizational assessment frameworks can be expressed in terms of a triad: organizational strategy, structure, and style. The appendix arrays ten representative schemes as a mix of these categories.

There seems to be something special about a triad. It represents a near-optimal balance of comprehensibility and complexity. Theoretical constructs containing four or more elements are notoriously difficult to retain. Three is manageable. At the same time, the number three gets us beyond binary thinking. We no longer have to be hung up in a dichotomous world in which one is either a "theory x" or a "theory y" manager, an authoritarian or a participative leader, a dictator or an abdicator. And no longer are the options simply team or non-team.

More basically, I am drawn to a triad because I believe there are three archetypal organization designs. These designs, which are mirrored by baseball, football, and basketball, can be arrayed as the vertices of an equilateral triangle—so that any mix of autonomy (baseball), control (football), and cooperation (basketball) can be plotted within. Actually, what prompted me to use this graphic was my exposure to the Maxwell "color triangle," whose vertices are the primary colors of light: red, blue, and green. Any conceivable color can be described by a point inside this triangle.[18]

To see organizational design in three dimensions is to view it in color, as opposed to black and white and shades

Figure 2.1. Three Organizational Designs

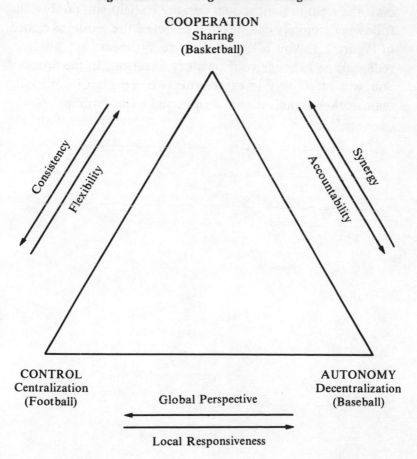

COOPERATION
Sharing
(Basketball)

Consistency

Flexibility

Accountability

Synergy

CONTROL
Centralization
(Football)

Global Perspective

AUTONOMY
Decentralization
(Baseball)

Local Responsiveness

of gray—the usual two-dimensional rendering. As Figure 2.1 shows, a three-dimensional portrayal clarifies the tradeoffs that every organization must repeatedly face.

What do you want your organization to excel at? No organization can be exceptional at everything. Good, perhaps, but not exceptional. For instance, if the effort is made to maximize consistency and flexibility simultaneously, organizational behavior will be neither highly consistent nor highly flexible, since each quality comes at the expense of the other.

The challenge is to line up priorities correctly and then to craft the right organizational design. To help you do this, the following chapters will develop in detail the model sketched in Figure 2.1. You will learn how to systematically analyze, redesign, and change your own organization. In the process, you will effectively integrate the two worlds of corporate teamwork—organizational design and team-building.

Chapter Three

The Teamwork Profile

The first step in characterizing your organization is to have a sound conceptual framework. The Teamwork Profile (Table 3.1) provides a systematic way to assess organizational strategy, structure, and style. The Profile presents three "ideal types" of organization—autonomy-based, control-based, and cooperation-based. You can use this framework to pattern your own organization's design as a blend of the ideal types. This chapter will set out the definitions and examples that can help you do this.

One of the strengths of this methodology is that it can be applied at any system level. In general, however, I recommend that the Profile be used first by the management team:

(1) To characterize the overall organization *as it is now* (Chapter 4)

(2) To characterize the organization *as it should be* (Chapter 6)

(3) To characterize the organization *as it will be* (Chapter 7)

I became a believer in top-first, if not top-down, change the hard way. During the mid-1970s, in collaboration with Eric Trist, John Eldred, Chris Meek, and Larry Carter, I consulted to more than 10 companies at the work-system level to develop productivity and quality of worklife programs. We discovered that often, the more successful a program was, the more vulnerable it became. Whether the content was work redesign, productivity gainsharing, or worker involvement in problem-solving, positive results were typically followed by negative consequences as people higher in the hierarchy became threatened about losing power and eventually sabotaged the experimental project. After a fair number of what I came to regard as "pitching wedge trajec-

Table 3.1 TEAMWORK PROFILE

	AUTONOMY (Baseball)	CONTROL (Football)	COOPERATION (Basketball)
ORGANIZATIONAL STRATEGY			
• Distinctive competence (What organizational competencies separate us from our competition?)	Adding value through star performers	Reducing costs and/or complexity through global coordination	Innovating by combining resources in novel ways
• Developmental pattern (How do we pursue development/ renewal/ growth?)	From the outside	From within	In concert with others
ORGANIZATIONAL STRUCTURE			
• Coordinating mechanism (How do we manage inter-dependence?)	Design of free-standing roles/ units	Hierarchical planning and administration	Mutual adjustment
• Decision system (Who is involved in decision-making, when, and in what ways?)	Decentralized	Centralized	Shared
• Information system (Who has access to the information necessary to make decisions?)	Locally controlled	Globally controlled	Distributed

(cont.)

Table 3.1 (Continued)

	AUTONOMY (Baseball)	CONTROL (Football)	COOPERATION (Basketball)
ORGANIZATIONAL STRUCTURE			
• Reward system (What behaviors are reinforced financially and nonfinancially?)	Individualistic	Hierarchic	Mutualistic
• Effect of physical configuration (What human interaction does our physical design encourage?)	Independent action	Programmed interaction	Spontaneous interaction
ORGANIZATIONAL STYLE			
• Organizational expectation (What does the organization expect from its people?)	Self-reliance	Compliance	Collaboration
• Individual expectation (What do people expect from their organization?)	Opportunity	Security	Community
• Cultural bias (What is our overriding social value?)	Diversity	Uniformity	Complementarity

tory" changes—fast up, high visibility, fast down, with very little ground covered (like a wedge shot in golf), I resolved to start at the top wherever possible—and hopefully, help clients hit 250-yard drives.

In fact, there is no such thing as a neat, linear, top-to-middle-to-bottom change process—which is one reason that I have difficulty with the expression "top-*down*." Once organizational change is in motion, it will trace routes that could not have been predicted; unless consciously checked, change will occur in vertical, horizontal, and diagonal directions all at once. Despite this complexity, however, it is possible to choose among alternate change trajectories. I opt for starting with senior management. This is where leverage resides.

Before analyzing the change process, it is important to explain the ten dimensions of the Teamwork Profile. This framework is deceptively simple.

ORGANIZATIONAL STRATEGY

An organization's strategy is its method of competing. Strategy has two components: how an organization actually competes now, and how it assures its capability of competing in the future.

Distinctive Competence

Virtuosos' Skills: Adding Value through Star Performers

Distinctive competence means competitive edge—those current capabilities that set an organization apart from all others. If it relies on individual/unit autonomy, an organization is a star system; it adds value through outstanding individual performances by its players. In general, organizations whose products or services are most differentiated and of the highest quality fit this pattern. They compete on the basis of finely developed individual skills. Their players are craftsmen, artists, scientists, scholars, or service professionals.

Anyone who has spent time at a prestigious research university knows that the autonomy of professors is inviolate. Just look at the familiar research products of such a system—journal articles, technical reports, and books. Most are authored by a single person, or perhaps two or three people. How to build a top-flight university? Shoot for the stars. Frederick Terman's concept of "steeples of excellence," the blueprint for making Stanford first-class, still makes sense. According to Terman, "Academic prestige depends upon high but narrow steeples of academic excellence, rather than upon coverage of more modest height extending solidly over a broad discipline." A steeple is "a small faculty group of experts in a narrow area of knowledge"—in other words, a team of academic heavy hitters.[1]

Individual autonomy is no less important to scientists outside university campuses. Bell Labs historically has operated "by ones and twos," according to vice president of research Arno Penzias.[2] The ones and twos have just happened to be world authorities in their disciplines. Research-based corporations like Merck & Co. understand the nature of their game and what it takes to succeed at it. In the words of Merck R&D Chief Dr. Edward M. Scolnick, "We tell people they control their own destiny. If you have bright, highly motivated people who feel responsible for their work, they will discover great things."[3]

Images of assembly lines notwithstanding, even the automobile industry provides ample examples of player autonomy. Companies such as Porsche, Mercedes-Benz, Lotus, and, of course, Rolls-Royce, depend on star engineers and craftsmen. A Lotus advertisement proclaims that firm's "stubborn individualism" and goes on to note that a Lotus engine "is unhurriedly assembled by hand, with all parts (right down to the valve springs) so carefully matched and balanced that it takes two full weeks to complete a single engine."

In fact, the products of autonomy-based organizations are apt to be differentiated from each other, as well as from the competition's products. Atlas Company of Boston, a maker of briefcases, advertises to stress just this point:

> PICASSO. VAN GOGH. MICHELANGELO.
> MEYER RHODES.
> You can always tell the hand of a master. And a fine leather case is like an original painting.
>
> Your Atlas case is an original—there's no other case like it in the world.
>
> Meyer Rhodes? He's one of the master craftsmen at Atlas who makes sure every case is like no other. Because he builds them. One at a time. By hand.
>
> Leather is an animal's skin, unique and natural. This individuality is why our leather cases are so special. And frankly, more expensive than others that have been stamped out of a mold.
>
> In synthetic materials such as vinyls and plastics and lesser quality leathers, you get absolute identity time after time. Only in fine leathers do you get an original every time.

There is typically a customized quality to the products of an autonomy-based organization, even when these are not consciously matched with the needs and idiosyncrasies of an individual customer or user. Architect/designer Christopher Alexander explains why, in terms of the housing market: "Personal and individual houses are always worth more than mass-produced houses. When you buy such a house, it fits you better, *not* because you are the person who created it, but simply because a *particular person* created it."[4]

As with products, so with services. Consider Morgan Stanley, the old-line investment banking firm. Even as it has ventured beyond its longtime staple, underwriting, and into more high-volume, low-fee areas such as commercial paper, Morgan has remained committed to competing on the basis of star performers. Thus, while its competitors may average five to six clients per salesperson, Morgan expects its salespersons to work with no more than two or three.[5]

In the insurance industry, a prime example of competing on the basis of individual stars is Fred Carr's First Executive Corporation. *Fortune* summed up Carr's strategy in a 1984 article: "First Executive's staff is the trimmest of any major underwriter's. With just 394 employees, the company writes as much insurance as outfits with 10 times the work force. It has wooed 400 top independent agents, who concentrate on selling large policies to rich individuals."[6]

A characteristic that appears to be common to all autonomy-oriented organizations is the player's identification with the product or service, with the customer, or with both. Alfred Lohner, a foreman who joined Mercedes-Benz in 1948, admits that "I feel personally connected to each car that goes by here."[7] At Cray Research, which makes $20 million supercomputers—"the Porsches of the computer industry," according to *Business Week*—the very idea of selling has been transformed. Says Marcelo Gumucio, Cray's executive vice-president for marketing: "We're not trying to sell a product.

We're trying to establish a relationship. It's a little like a marriage."[8]

In a widely-circulated advertisement, Arthur Young likens itself to Hillerich & Bradsby, maker of the famous Louisville Slugger® baseball bat—each one individually tailored to a player's needs: "Arthur Young understands what customized service can mean to a client. That's why we get personally involved with our clients before we give them an ounce of financial advice. After all, the more we know about their business, the more we can help them."

Another characteristic of at least many, if not all, organizations that emphasize individual autonomy is a relative absence of time pressure in delivering the product or service. It takes six weeks to build a Lotus. Three months to build a Rolls-Royce. To sell a Cray supercomputer may take five years. Then, of course, there are the worlds of discovery and invention, of basic research and academe. Basic research, as opposed to applied research, is not concerned with specific commercial applications; such work may have a time frame of 20 to 30 years. Similarly, university professors' areas of inquiry occupy them for a lifetime. Donald Rose, a Ph.D. in applied mathematics who went from Bell Labs to Duke University in 1984, summed it up nicely: "Research needs time where people can go away and do pointy-headed things."[9]

Control from on High:
Reducing Costs and/or Complexity
through Global Coordination

The "opposite" of reliance on star individual performers is a control-orientation in which authority, information, and initiative reside at the top of the organization. The distinctive competence of such an organization is its ability to reduce costs and/or complexity through hierarchical planning and coordinating. While an autonomy-based organization tends to maximize the positives, a control-based organization minimizes the negatives. Cost-reduction techniques are often used abundantly. To wit: put more R&D dollars into process improvements than into product enhancements; use modular product components wherever possible; minimize the material content of products; minimize the number of parts; use inexpensive materials (e.g., recycled versus virgin paper or metal); produce in high volumes.

In general, the products or services of a highly-controlled organization are less differentiated than those of an organization that emphasizes individual autonomy. Thus, a large community college is not designed to generate original research, any more than it is set up to respond sensitively to the peculiarities of each and every student. Rather, its forte is the ability to deliver a predictable and consistent educational package to a large number of students at an affordable price. The key skill here is the administration's ability to manage the logistics of large numbers—of students.

By far the most powerful example and symbol of a control-based organization is the classic automobile assembly line, in which every step of a cumulative, long-linked production process is carefully orchestrated from above. The service sector has no dearth of equivalents, probably the most famous of which is McDonald's. McDonald's is dedicated to making every hamburger look, taste, smell, and feel the same, whether it's served in New York, New Mexico, or New Zealand. Lest consistency suffer, opportunities for workers to improvise on the job have all but been eliminated.

McDonald's assembly-line approach to service has been widely copied. The car oil change/lubrication business, for instance, now features Jiffy Lube, Minit-Lube, and a host of other chains—all of which are trying to offer our cars the equivalent of what McDonald's offers us: a consistent product, low cost, efficient service, and cleanliness.[10] There is no small irony in the circularity here: McDonald's applied automobile manufacturing concepts to servicing people; now the oil change/lube outfits are consciously aping McDonald's in order to take the same concepts back to servicing automobiles.

Hyatt Legal Services is yet another variation on the control theme. By streamlining and standardizing the practice of law, Hyatt has elected to compete as a high-volume, low-cost player. How to make money in this game? Says financial backer Robert Bass, "The key is to manage very tightly."[11]

In financial services, the near-opposite of Fred Carr's First Executive Corporation is Arthur Williams' A. L. Williams, which uses a huge complement of part-timers to sell term insurance, chiefly to lower-middle income people who currently have whole-life policies. According to *Forbes*, the Williams sales organization "is like an army of hastily trained recruits where several cadres of skilled and highly paid sales professionals command masses of foot soldiers."[12]

A control-based strategy is required not just for high-volume production and service delivery; it is necessary whenever a long train of activities must be carefully sequenced in a particular way. If you're going to build a bridge over a river, the last thing you want to do is to delegate the job to one person on the west bank and another on the east bank with the hope that they will somehow meet at the middle of the river. Indeed, for virtually all complex construction or engineering projects—like dams, canals, and highway systems—global perspective and top-down control are essential.

The consistency that top-down control makes possible is sometimes more important for safety reasons than for purely economic ones. New-drug development by pharmaceutical companies, for instance, must be tightly monitored because of possible toxic and/or carcinogenic side effects. Similarly, the generation of nuclear power is sufficiently dangerous that it must be regulated from above—by government—even if this means ruling out autonomous local experimentation that could accelerate learning. The price of failure is prohibitive.[13]

In contrast to his or her counterpart in an autonomy-based organization, the player in a control-based organization is unlikely to identify strongly with either product or customer. Instead, the individual will tend to relate more to his own organization, in particular to that part of it—work crew, department, facility, whatever—to which he belongs. In fact, the individual may only dimly comprehend larger organizational purpose and the connection between this purpose and his or her own work and unit—although he or she may identify vicariously with the power that the larger organization symbolizes.

Time pressures typically exert a powerful influence on the members of a control-oriented organization. It's less a matter of having to run flat out than of conforming to externally imposed paces, routines, or deadlines. Because this kind of organization, in principle at least, tries to approximate a machine, each of its parts must submit to hierarchically developed schedules. It is the preparer of such schedules—the designer of global protocols—and the manager who directs implementation who are the "stars" in a control-based organization. This arrangement is the converse of an autonomy-based organization, where the stars are clearly the players.

A simple way to reinforce the contrast was suggested to me by a question I am frequently asked: "What's the difference between the player on an autonomy-based team and the coach or manager of a control-based team? Aren't they really the same thing?" Not quite. The contrast is equivalent to artist versus architect. Architects conceive designs, which are then implemented, or "built," by subordinate others. Artists, in contrast, carry out both design and implementation themselves; they are involved physically as well as conceptually.

Another difference is worth noting. An artist creates a painting or sculpture or song that people can "consume" or not. People are usually not constrained by the art form; by and large they can take it or leave it. Less so with an architect's product. A building necessarily constrains those in it and, indeed, those who come near it. The product of a control-based organization is similarly constraining to the extent that it requires people to adapt to it, rather than vice versa. Henry Ford's monochromatic Model T—available in any color so long as it's black—was a famous case in point. Ironically, so were General Motors' undifferentiated cars of the mid-1980s.

Creative Blends: Innovating by Combining Resources in Novel Ways

An organization that emphasizes cooperation competes on the basis of its ability to innovate by putting together resources in new ways. It may have an edge in costs, as do steel minimills like Nucor Corp. Or it may make high-value-added products, as does Electro Scientific Industries, Inc., a manufacturer of laser trimming devices, among other things. Or it may emphasize novelty, flexibility, or service to its customers. But whatever the external competitive advantage, the distinctive competence that drives such an organization is innovation through cooperation.

An example of a cooperation-based organization with academic roots is the Wharton Center for Applied Research, until recently a part of the University of Pennsylvania. The Center concentrates on problems for which there are no off-the-shelf solutions; such problems typically require bringing together specialists from several academic disciplines. As the Center's brochure states, "Some of our most successful projects involve multi-disciplinary combinations. . . . Our strength is in our ability to combine expertise in many functional areas to design unique and practical solutions."

An autonomy strategy provides local responsiveness; a control strategy, global perspective. A cooperation strategy can sometimes integrate these polar points of view. In the early- to mid-1980s, Honeywell's control systems group faced a situation in which customers on the one hand demanded customized solutions—typically involving multiple products—yet insisted on dealing with a single, unified supplier. In other words, Honeywell's customers expected both a high level of sensitivity to their distinctive needs (local responsiveness) and a high degree of technological integration (global perspective). Honeywell responded with an initiative it called "Cross Corporate Collaboration": Different divisions and account representatives became responsible for voluntarily "working together to maximize business opportunities with existing targeted customers in their geographic market."[14]

If the automobile industry—historically so control-oriented—can provide examples of individual autonomy (like Rolls-Royce and Porsche), it can likewise supply cases of voluntary cooperation. The most dramatic such demonstration is Volvo's Kalmar plant, which has been in operation since 1974. Kalmar effectively replaced the long-linked logic of the assembly line with several 20-person groups, each responsible for assembling an entire car subsystem, such as the electrical system, wheels and brakes, or interior. Each work group sets its own pace and allocates work among its members, most of whom have chosen to learn multiple skills. Volvo is taking the non-assembly-line concept even further with its Uddevalla plant, due on line in late 1988. Here the plan is for each work team to assemble an entire automobile.[15]

One of the most convincing demonstrations that cooperation can yield innovation comes from the world of advertising. Historically, an ad would first be conceived by a copywriter, who would then pass the language on to a lower-status artist. William Bernbach, co-founder of Doyle Dane Bernbach, changed the game. He forced copywriter and artist to work together, as equals, in a dynamic exchange in which the final product would be something greater than the sum of the words and the lines. The quality of the ads generated by this interactive process gained Bernbach a reputation as one of the "fathers" of creative advertising.[16]

Voluntary cooperation is prevalent in high-technology companies if for no other reason than the rapid development of new knowledge—and the consequent need for people from different technical specialties to share information. Cooperation-based organizations often have to work at a fever pitch, especially if their charter is applied research—the commercialization of a product or service. Applied research is to basic research as innovation is to invention. No open-ended ivory-tower reveries for those whose job is application/innovation. But the time pressures that a cooperation-based organization faces also differ—in kind more than in degree—from those confronted by a control-based organization. Even though their pace may be faster, the players in a cooperation-based organization retain at least some control over this factor.

In general, members of cooperation-based organizations identify more with the process of working together than do their counterparts in either autonomy- or control-based organizations. Autonomy implies the exercise of leadership *by* organizational players—individually. Control implies top-down leadership *of* players by the coach (manager). Cooperation implies leadership that is distributed *among* the players, and *between* players and coach. The prepositional differences are crucial. In a cooperation-based organization, players-and-coach as a unit are the star.

Developmental Pattern

Buyers: From the Outside

Growth is quantitative; it has to do with "more" or "bigger." Development is qualitative; in Russell Ackoff's words, it is "an increase in capability and competence."[17] Most corporations are concerned with growth; all should be concerned with development. But how to express these concerns varies. At one extreme, an organization may grow and/or develop in large measure by acquiring outside resources—including human resources. Conglomerates typically follow this tack. But so do many nonconglomerates. MCI, for example, has a policy that 40 percent of the job openings at every level must be filled by outsiders. CEO Bill McGowan believes that this requirement ensures a steady stream of new blood to challenge entrenched practices. The policy also helps MCI to simulate a free market environment. States McGowan: "We even encourage people to leave the company for a while by allowing them to come back without sacrificing their benefits, their credits for prior service in things like vacations and pensions. We also have no prohibition on one department trying to take away the best people in another department."[18]

Universities are notorious for bringing in professors from the outside. Some of the most publicized examples involve famous schools' efforts to recruit academic stars, so-called "matinee-idol" faculty. But the game isn't limited to the top tier. John Corson, a former Princeton professor who resigned from the Board of Regents at Virginia's George Mason University, admitted that such a plan—which he opposed—had worked for George Mason: "I couldn't accept the philosophy that you could go out and buy people the way you might hire auto mechanics. But they seem to have pulled it off."[19]

Makers: From Within

The opposite extreme is to develop/grow entirely from within. Companies following this route seldom bring in new people for other than entry-level positions. Nor do they acquire other resources from the outside, preferring instead to home-grow their own. Firms like Caterpillar and Kodak, at least into the early 1980s, typified this pattern, in which the goal was to be as self-contained and self-sufficient as possible.

A 1984 *Forbes* article notes that ever since a supplier's critical error in 1880 (a faulty gelatin base that led to the failure of photographic plates), "Kodak has determined not to rely on outsiders, for loans or anything else. Its . . . chemical business is an outgrowth of . . . George Eastman's decision to ensure the supply of the chemical feedstocks needed to make film. Kodak Park, the huge main plant in Rochester, N.Y., has its own fire department and power plant so that it is not dependent on the city. The company even makes its own cardboard and fabricates the boxes for its film. With fat profits, it was long able to integrate backward and at the same time develop new products from within without going deeply into debt."[20]

Joint Ventures: In Concert with Others

The third alternative falls outside the extremes just outlined. Development and concomitant growth become reconceptualized as less a matter of buy-versus-make than of collaborating with others. One insurance firm cited by Russell Ackoff articulated the following human resources principle as a guide to future development: "The enterprise should take advantage of other resources available outside the enterprise by utilizing outside consultants and cooperative ventures where this would aid efficient and effective operations."[21]

The tendency to work with others is increasingly evident among science-based companies because, as Control Data's chairman Robert M. Price has argued, "Technology is so complex and changing so rapidly that no one company can maintain all the necessary R&D resources."[22] Consortia like Microelectronics & Computer Technology Corp. (MCC) and Bell Communications Research Inc. (Bellcore) are representative of the trend.

For those who would like to track a matched philosophical pair—make it ourselves versus work in concert with others—Korea's Hyundai and Daewoo offer a near-perfect contrast. Hyundai under founder/chairman Chung Ju-Yung is highly integrated, control-oriented, and insular; it wants little to do with outsiders, especially non-Koreans. On the other hand, Daewoo under founder/chairman Kim Woo-Choong openly solicits partners; as of late 1986 Daewoo had no fewer than 34 technical-cooperation agreements and seven joint ventures, representing a U.S. investment of perhaps $400 million.[23]

ORGANIZATIONAL STRUCTURE

The right organizational strategy is essential to high performance, but it is hardly sufficient. Unless organizational structure is properly matched with strategy, performance will suffer. Structure is a combination of coordinating mechanism, multiple systems, and geography.

Coordinating Mechanism

This dimension is the primary means used to manage *interdependence*—that is, work flows and information flows among organizational units. There are three kinds of interdependence: pooled, sequential, and reciprocal.[24] In pooled interdependence, organizational parts are relatively independent of each other; each part provides a discrete contribution to the corporate whole. In sequential interdependence, organizational parts interact in series; each renders a cumulative contribution to the corporate whole. In reciprocal interdependence, the parts interact in a back-and-forth manner and make joint contributions to the corporate whole. The three forms of interdependence are illustrated in Figure 3.1.

In Parallel: Design of Free-Standing Roles/Units

Coordinating through the design of free-standing roles/units amounts to reducing the need for coordination. Each part—role or unit—is self-contained; it has virtually all the resources required to carry out its tasks, and has little need to interact with other parts or with the corporate office. Thus, the interdependence among parts is pooled. A geographically

Figure 3.1. Three Patterns of Interdependence

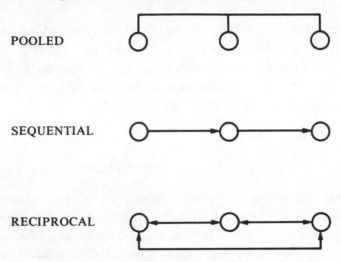

POOLED

SEQUENTIAL

RECIPROCAL

organized firm like Cray Research, which in 1986 was divided into four domestic regions—each with its own board of directors, and run like an independent entity—exemplifies this pattern. So does a conglomerate or holding company made up of several disparate operating businesses.

When coordination is achieved through design, each unit is, at least theoretically, a discrete profit center. Thus, in 1985, Georgia-Pacific had more than 400 profit centers. Profit-center managers there are responsible not only for running their operations effectively; they are also expected to manage working capital effectively. To this end, the corporation charges each profit center interest on the working capital the latter employs.[25]

In Series: Hierarchical Planning and Administration

Coordinating by hierarchical planning and administration is a pattern associated with organizations whose major parts must be carefully meshed. Single-product and dominant-product firms—like Wrigley and, until recently, Maytag—have for decades relied on hierarchical authority.

Hierarchical coordination fits sequential interdependence, especially where the organization's activities form a long-linked, essentially one-way chain. This is clearly the case with vertically integrated corporations, such as major oil companies whose activities span crude-oil discovery, production, transportation, refining, and marketing. The longer the sequence of activities, the steeper the hierarchy tends to be. Indeed, the management hierarchy often appears to be a vertical mirror of the horizontal chain of linked organizational units. Or, viewed in a somewhat different light, we tend to find more hierarchical levels, and fewer profit centers, than in an organization based on the design of free-standing parts. Perhaps there is some numerical tradeoff between hierarchical levels and profit centers.

Back-and-Forth: Mutual Adjustment

The third kind of coordinating mechanism is mutual adjustment—voluntary cooperation among organizational parts. This pattern is required when interaction among parts (1) is critical (thus ruling out the design of free-standing roles/units) but (2) must take place in a rapidly-changing and/or complex environment (that exceeds the response capacity of hierarchy). Patterns of mutual adjustment are horizontal and diagonal. They are also likely both to run counter to (as well as in the direction of) work flow and to cut across lines of authority.

Probably the most celebrated corporate examples of mutual adjustment have come from high-tech electronics and computer companies, such as Digital Equipment, Hewlett-

Packard, Intel, Tandem Computers, Tektronix, Xerox. In such firms, intense needs to share information and resources, both within and across divisions, have led to fluid patterns of coordination.

Not surprisingly, organizations that emphasize nonhierarchical forms of coordination, either by designing freestanding units or by relying on mutual adjustment, tend to be flatter—to have fewer hierarchical levels—than those that rely on hierarchy. Nonhierarchical coordinating mechanisms minimize the need for top-down control and therefore, the rationale for a steep pyramid. However, it should be noted that flatter organizations are not *necessarily* always less centrally controlled than steeper ones. As both Peter Drucker and Jay Galbraith have pointed out, (vertical) information systems represent a functional substitute for hierarchy. By investing heavily in such a system, an organization can retain its tautness while doing away with a number of hierarchical levels. In effect, computers replace human coordinators.

Decision System

Every decision system is a blend of three processes: decentralization, centralization, and sharing. These contrasting patterns are summarized in Figure 3.2.

Delegate: Decentralized

Decentralization—delegation—is common in book publishing. Editors often delegate a great deal to their authors. Phyllis Grann, president of G. P. Putnam's Sons, is a highly respected editor, but she never tries to impose her ideas on authors: "I never argue. . . . I say, hey, it's your book. I get

Figure 3.2. Three Patterns of Decision-Making

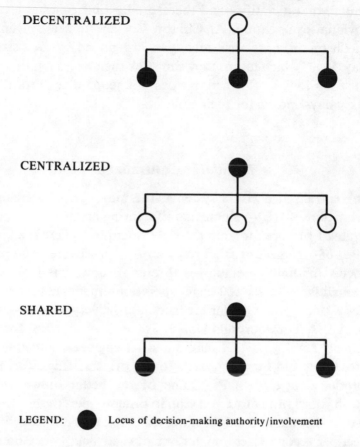

DECENTRALIZED

CENTRALIZED

SHARED

LEGEND: Locus of decision-making authority/involvement

paid to do my homework. That's the service I supply to you. What you do with it is up to you.''[26]

Decentralized decision systems are risk-embracing. They are likely to encourage swinging for the fences. Winning under such conditions may amount to relative failure—just as a successful hitter in baseball fails two-thirds of the time, and a successful slugger fails even more often. (Babe Ruth struck out almost two times for every home run he hit.) One index of a risk-embracing posture may be the presence of rules of thumb that quantify—and therefore legitimize—what an individual can venture. At Chilton Corporation, a consumer credit reporting service, managers are guided by the "sixty-day rule," which means they can stick their necks out on new ideas so long as this action does not jeopardize more than sixty days' profit for their unit.[27]

Mandate: Centralized

In centralized decision systems, the major shots are called from above. High-volume manufacturing and vertically integrated firms are far from the only examples. There is a large class of organizations that rely on rules, procedures, and protocols for limiting employee discretion down the line. McDonald's, with its 600-page operations manual, heads the list. Conceptually similar are trucking/delivery concerns such as A-P-A Transport and United Parcel Service. UPS, for instance, employs over 1,000 industrial engineers to detail instructions and time standards for its drivers. This effort has produced myriad SOPs. Some of the better-known ones: Beep your horn before you stop in order to alert the customer (so he'll come to the door more quickly); cover at least three feet per second after you get out of the truck; knock on the front door before wasting time trying to find the doorbell.[28]

Chicago Research & Trading Group, a large futures and options trading firm, also sends in the plays from the sideline. Its traders diligently follow printouts that specify prices at which to buy and sell. Jf conditions change materially, a new printout is provided. Observes a competitor: "They take away the individual decision-making from their floor traders. That makes for very nonemotional trading."[29]

Centralized decision systems are risk-averse. Such a bias

describes the traditional American approach to production, in which, as some academics have put it, every effort must go into "sealing off the technical core" of the company—that is, ensuring that no organizational disruptions or environmental perturbations affect product flow through the factory. A risk-averse style regards risks as essentially negative. No wonder ITT's Harold Geneen yearned for a world of no surprises: Just as most football coaches believe that "football games are not won, they're lost," Geneen believed that "Ninety-nine percent of all surprises in business are negative."[30]

Collaborate: Shared

With decentralization, the manager delegates. With centralization, he or she mandates. When decision-making is shared, the manager collaborates. Collaboration may take either of two forms: consultation or consensus. With consultation, a manager solicits input from subordinates (or peers) before reaching a decision. With consensus, manager and subordinates/peers jointly arrive at a decision.

Shared decision systems tend to be risk-accepting. This posture is perhaps most common in fast-changing situations in which a substantial degree of risk must be confronted even though the whole organization may suffer if things go badly—because it is not possible to seal off the risk-taking part from the rest of the organization. The more rapidly a firm's product life-cycles shrink, the greater the propensity for risk that is required—and at the same time, the greater the company's vulnerability. Hewlett-Packard, for instance, introduced no fewer than 23 varieties of electronic calculator between 1972 (its initial offering) and 1980. There is simply no way to make it in such a dynamic environment without some measure of risk-taking. Yet such firms have to hedge their bets.

W. L. Gore & Associates, which manufactures a synthetic fiber called Gore-Tex®, balances its risks by means of a procedure it applies to "waterline decisions." Typically at Gore, employees, or "associates" as they are called, are free to decide things on their own. But when confronted with a waterline decision, one which "could twist toward the company's waterline"[31]—that is, threaten to capsize the firm—associates are expected to consult with others.

Coordinating mechanism and decision system are complementary dimensions; the former refers to *horizontal* work/information flows, the latter to *vertical* authority patterns.[32] Figure 3.3 combines these dimensions in terms of interdependence and decision-making.

Information System

Where the Action Is: Locally Controlled

The key questions are: what information is needed, by whom, and when, in order for effective decisions to be made? A locally controlled information system is one in which each person or unit has its own data base and the freedom to manipulate it. At the extreme, the organization is comprised of hundreds or even thousands of discrete data bases, each perhaps tied to a minicomputer or a personal computer (PC). Thus, many sales and consulting organizations are made up of dispersed individuals who have little need to communicate with one another, and equally little reason to access a global database.

Figure 3.3. Combined Patterns of Interdependence and Decision-Making

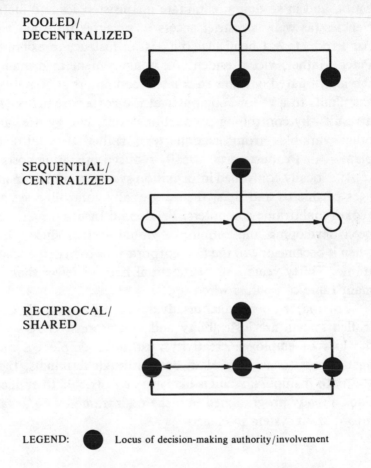

POOLED/
DECENTRALIZED

SEQUENTIAL/
CENTRALIZED

RECIPROCAL/
SHARED

LEGEND: Locus of decision-making authority/involvement

The Big Picture: Globally Controlled

A locally controlled information system can be attuned to local conditions and able to respond without delay. But its perspective will always be limited. It may also duplicate resources and lead to serious differences in information and procedures across the company. In contrast, a globally controlled information system can encompass the whole organization and in so doing, eliminate inconsistencies and inefficiencies (as well as restrict access to sensitive information). Air Products & Chemicals, Inc., is an instructive example. Peter Mather, vice-president for management information services, figured out how to connect computers at 80 natural gas plants to a central computer at the corporate office. As a result—by controlling production levels, energy use, and other variables from headquarters, rather than at each plant—Air Products dramatically reduced operating costs.[33]

If a locally controlled information system conjures up images of micros and PCs, then a globally controlled system evokes mainframe computers. Prudential Insurance Co. has been developing and refining a global system since 1955, when it became one of the first corporations to install a mainframe. Thirty years later, Prudential had no fewer than 25 mainframe computers wired up.

The major operational disadvantages of a centrally controlled system are inflexibility and nonresponsiveness—and the loss of employee creativity. Although employees may have access to a global data base through terminals, their ability to manipulate data is likely to be restricted to applications already programmed into the mainframe by corporate information system managers.

On-Line, Real-Time: Distributed

A distributed information system combines global perspective with local access and initiative. Such a system may link mainframes and PCs. Thus, Travelers Corporation in late 1987 had some 20,000 PCs connected to 14 mainframe computers. A different variety of distributed system is one based on a local area network (LAN), in which multifunctional workstations share information without recourse to a mainframe.

Xerox Corporation pioneered in distributed systems by developing the technology for Ethernet network, which made it possible to move information among different machines. More recently, Xerox's efforts to link geographically distant worksites are a particularly important example because they are as concerned with psychosocial relations as with technology. *The Wall Street Journal* describes aspects of the Xerox project, begun in 1985, to design an electronic office-of-the-future: "The all-day video and audio connections [at each site] make a big difference, letting the offices interrelate casually as well as formally. The main links connect the common areas at the center of both labs, each of which has a camera, a big-screen video monitor and a speaker phone. Everyone typically passes under those cameras' gazes several times a day."[34]

Apart from any fears about Big Brother-type surveillance that may be prompted by futuristic electronic offices, more routine distributed information systems are not without their drawbacks. On the surface, a *completely* distributed system sounds wonderful: data that are global in scope yet manipulable in real time by anybody. At the limit, everyone in touch with everyone else—just as in an electronic office. What could possibly be wrong with such an arrangement? First, obviously, is the cost of building and maintaining the system. Second is the cost to the individual (also a cost to the organization) in the form of information overload. As Russell Ackoff has observed, most managers have a greater need for *less irrelevant information* than for *more relevant information*. They need dampeners, not resonators.

Ackoff points out another, more subtle difficulty related to overload on the organization: "unconstrained communication within corporations can improve their performance *only when their parts are not in conflict*—when their objectives are compatible and mutually reinforcing. It is apparent that in war the more opponents know about one another, the more harm they can inflict. If each side knew absolutely nothing about the other, war could not be waged. It is commonplace for parts of a corporation to be at war among themselves, or in competition."[35]

Reward System

Pay for Superstars: Individualistic

The final "system" for our purposes is concerned with the rewards—financial and nonfinancial—that organizational members receive. An individualistic reward system is oriented to the star player, irrespective of his or her location in the organizational hierarchy. Pay, perks, and promotion reflect performance.

With an individualistic system, meeting competitors' pay levels is more important than fitting some internal compensation structure. Understandably, individual or unit incentives figure prominently. At H.J. Heinz Co., roughly two thirds of the pay earned by the top 300 managers is based on performance incentives. In the words of CEO Anthony J. F. O'Reilly, "You don't get very much for just coming to work here. We lag behind 27 peer companies—we are the lowest—in base compensation. We pay a large short-term management incentive package and we pay a *very* large long-term incentive package."[36]

With an individualistic reward system, it is not unusual for people to be pitted against each other. For instance at conglomerate Textron, under founder Royal Little, division managers were rank-ordered each month by performance.

Organizational Structure

Domino's Pizza, Inc., ranks its stores weekly by gross sales. At Merrill Lynch, in 1983 a single star broker brought in more than $4 million in commissions (earning himself over $1.5 million) at the same time that that firm was trying to rid itself of brokers unable to garner gross annual commissions of at least $250,000. A similar philosophy—if less extreme in numbers—is taking hold at GE. Explained one official recently: "We want to reward superstars very well and reward routine performance routinely."[37]

Stock brokers, real estate brokers, investment bankers, insurance salespersons, management consultants, highly autonomous managers—all tend to thrive under individualistic pay schemes that reward long-ball hitters. Often, such stars make more than their bosses. At Bally Manufacturing in the mid-1980s, 18 people, all attached to quasi-autonomous units, made more than Chairman Robert E. Mullane's $592,222. Mullane's response? "I'm not eleemosynary, mind you. This is what's best for the company. I live very nicely. I like my job. Should I be upset when I go to the ball park and the pitcher is making $2 million?"[38] Mullane picked the right sport as his metaphor. Baseball has always had the largest number of big earners. The immortal Babe Ruth summed things up in 1931 with his immortal reaction to why his $80,000 salary should exceed (by $5,000) that of President Herbert Hoover: "I had a better year."

Respect Rank: Hierarchic

A hierarchic reward system lines everyone up by vertical location in the organizational pyramid. Since virtually everything about a control-oriented organization is designed to achieve machinelike precision, the reward system closely follows the authority system. Comparisons are typically internal, with other organizational positions, rather than external, with competitive equivalents. Rarely will an individual earn more than his or her boss.

As one might expect, hierarchic reward systems have a lot more levels to them than other varieties. In 1986, Caterpillar Inc. and the United Auto Workers negotiated a new contract that incorporated "significant" reductions of job classifications. The streamlined package for Peoria plants called for no fewer than 150 categories. To put this number in perspective, however, consider the prior number: 418.[39]

One of the more enduring hierarchic systems is the federal civil service's General Schedule (Table 3.2), which in 1987 was made up of 18 grades, each containing 10 steps.

Table 3.2. A HIERARCHIC REWARD SYSTEM

1987 FEDERAL GENERAL SCHEDULE (GS) PAY CHART

Steps	1	2	3	4	5	6	7	8	9	10
GS-1	$9.619	$9.940	$10.260	$10.579	$10.899	$11.087	$11.403	$11.721	$11.735	$12.036
2	10.816	11.073	11.430	11.735	11.866	12.215	12.564	12.913	13.262	13.611
3	11.802	12.195	12.588	12.981	13.374	13.767	14.160	14.553	14.946	15.339
4	13.248	13.690	14.132	14.574	15.016	15.458	15.900	16.342	16.784	17.226
5	14.822	15.316	15.810	16.304	16.798	17.292	17.786	18.280	18.774	19.268
6	16.521	17.072	17.623	18.174	18.725	19.276	19.827	20.378	20.929	21.480
7	18.358	18.970	19.582	20.194	20.806	21.418	22.030	22.642	23.254	23.866
8	20.333	21.011	21.689	22.367	23.045	23.723	24.401	25.079	25.757	26.435
9	22.458	23.207	23.956	24.705	25.454	26.203	26.952	27.701	28.450	29.199
10	24.732	25.556	26.380	27.204	28.028	28.852	29.676	30.500	31.324	32.148
11	27.172	28.078	28.984	29.890	30.796	31.702	32.808	33.514	34.420	35.326
12	32.567	33.653	34.739	35.825	36.911	37.997	39.083	40.169	41.255	42.341
13	38.727	40.018	41.309	42.600	43.891	45.182	46.473	47.764	49.055	50.346
14	45.763	47.288	48.813	50.338	51.863	53.388	54.913	56.438	57.963	59.488
15	53.830	55.624	57.418	59.212	61.006	62.800	64.594	66.388	68.182	69.976
16	63.135	65.240	67.345	69.450	71.555*	73.660*	75.765*	77.870*	79.975*	
17	73.958*	76.423*	78.888*	81.353*	83.818*					
18	86.682*									

*The rate of basic pay payable to employees at these rates is limited to the rate payable for level V of the Executive Schedule which would be $70,000.

Status symbols also tend to reflect hierarchy. The elite floor, the corner office, the Oriental rug, and the mahogany desk all match the organization chart. Probably the most blatant—and blatantly absurd—demonstration of this pattern that I have ever encountered occurred in the federal government in the 1970s. While I was consulting to the U.S. Office of Personnel Management, I came across a policy memorandum that inveighed against office furniture "miscegenation"—that is, the indiscriminate mixing of wood and metal furniture. Horrors!

In fact, in many "executive rows," the arrangement of senior corporate managers matches the firm's power structure. Such a scheme is in contrast to an individualistic reward system, in which status symbols separate people horizontally, not vertically: broker versus broker, consultant versus consultant, and so on. Indeed, the top salesperson may well have posher quarters than the company president, just as the star professor's digs may outclass those of the dean.

Spread the Wealth: Mutualistic

Mutualistic reward systems are neither extremely hierarchic nor extremely individualistic, and the span between highest- and lowest-paid tends to be less than in the other reward systems.

Consumers United Group, a Washington (DC)-based insurance company, is an unusual example. Here the minimum annual salary in 1987 was $18,000, and the maximum no more than three times that amount. Consumers United is worker-owned, and everyone shares profits equally.[40]

The emphasis with mutualistic reward systems is on stimulating working together. At the Legal Sea Foods restaurants in the Boston area, the paper placemats tell diners whom to seek for help: "our waiters and waitresses are trained to work as a team in order to better serve you. You needn't look for the person who initially took your order for additional help, just ask anyone. Gratuities are pooled among our waitering staff and divided equally. This is why you'll often find more than one person delivering your food. When any item is ready, the closest available people will serve you.''

Even individualistic Wall Street has its mutualistic exceptions. Perhaps most notable is Goldman Sachs, whose compensation system, according to senior partner John Weinberg, is designed to pull people together, rather than to set them apart from each other. Reports *Forbes*: ''Employees can earn as much in operations jobs as in the more glamorous mergers and acquisitions division. Traders can earn as much as investment bankers. Bonuses often are based on team results or on the firm's overall results rather than individual performance. This may disgruntle star producers but makes for highly efficient teamwork.''[41]

Mutualistic systems often feature the same bonus formula for everyone, as is the case at Pacific Telesis Group (PacTel), Woodward Governor Co., and Nucor Corp., the steelmaker. Hierarchic systems, by contrast, tend to reward higher-ups according to a more generous recipe, as has historically been the case at General Motors.

Mutualism means sharing pain as well as gain. Managers are expected to take cuts along with workers—a pattern especially noticeable among Japanese manufacturers such as Nissan Motor Corp. and Nippon Steel. At North Carolina-based Nucor, according to CEO F. Kenneth Iverson, ''Every employee in the company is on a bonus, and when business drops it is the officers' pay that takes the biggest hit.''[42]

The sharpest contrasts between hierarchic and mutualistic approaches may be found in those rust-belt twin towers, autos and steel. In an article titled ''A Tale of Two Worlds,'' *Forbes* contrasts two Ohio auto plants, the Jeep Division of American Motors and Honda of America.[43] The difference can be summed up by noting the distinctiveness of Honda: Employees—all of them—are called "associates"; all wear white coveralls bearing first names; all offices are open; all parking spaces are unreserved; all eat in the same cafeteria; and most significantly, all—workers and managers—view themselves as one.

Nucor exhibits many of the same qualities as Honda. But the root difference between this minimill company and the old-line, integrated steel producers is symbolized by color. In the conventional steel works, one finds a rainbow hierarchy: a power/status system denoted by the color of people's hardhats. At Nucor, one finds hardhats of a single hue: the color of money.

Effect of Physical Configuration

Whom in your neighborhood do you most often visit? Chances are it's the people next door, across the street, or in back of your house. Herbert Gans, author of *The Levittowners*, discovered from a survey of a tract development that 91 percent of all visiting involved people next door or directly across the street.[44] Thomas Allen of MIT reached a similar conclusion concerning communication patterns among R&D staff in industry: The probability that people five meters apart would communicate once or more a week was 25 percent; for people 10 meters away from each other, the probability dropped to 8 to 9 percent.[45]

Differences in interaction patterns are even more severe for vertical distances. Christopher Alexander has estimated that one flight of stairs is equivalent to about 100 horizontal feet and two flights of stairs to 300 horizontal feet. He concludes that units separated by two or more floors will have almost no informal contact with each other.[46] Location, location, location. It can be crucial.

Fly Solo: Independent Action

Some physical configurations encourage separateness and, therefore, independent action. If people or units have little or no need to interact with each other or with the corporate office, physical distances between them can be functional. Such has long been the case with sales forces, especially where different individuals are responsible for different territories. Likewise, R&D—in particular, basic R&D—is often best carried out far away from the corporate gaze. Telecommuting—and the phenomenon of computer commuters—is a recent development that reiterates this pattern.

March in Step: Programmed Interaction

By contrast, other configurations produce programmed interaction among people or units. Most high-volume manufacturing and service layouts do this. So do office arrangements in which managers and other employees are situated— usually by level and/or function—so that only certain exchanges normally take place (and by implication, certain others do not).

Mingle Informally: Spontaneous Interaction

A third type of physical configuration reinforces spontaneous interaction. Japanese companies are famous for locating engineers and other technical people right alongside the factory floor in order to maximize informal exchanges between these individuals and production workers. Xerox has achieved a similar effect with trainees through the design of its training facility in Virginia: the zigzag pattern that hallways trace through lounges makes it likely that students will bump into each other—although in no particular (programmed) pattern.

ORGANIZATIONAL STYLE

Style is strategy-and-structure's complement; it is the composite of subjective processes that blend with objective design features to define the nature of an organization. In fact, the lines between strategy and structure and style are always blurred, and several dimensions could just as easily be grouped under any of these headings.

Organizational Expectation

Make Up Your Own Mind:
Self-reliance

An organization that puts a premium on self-reliance wants employees to be self-starters, to take the initiative. At companies like Raychem Corporation, for example, every person—including new hires—is expected to find his or her own way. One is reminded of major league pitcher Gaylord Perry's observation about baseball: "Do for yourself or do without."

Consultant Stanley Davis relates a story about Ned Johnson, CEO and son of the founder of Fidelity Management and Research Corporation. During a panel on corporate culture, Johnson became ever more certain that Fidelity lacked one, "because every one of our managers does his own thing and is measured by the growth of his own fund. There is no one Fidelity culture." Davis goes on to explain that Johnson's father was committed to the principle of placing "responsibility for a fund's management with an individual and never with an investment committee. Thus the guiding principle was individual performance."[47] In other words, Fidelity had a very powerful culture that was based on the organizational expectation of self-reliance.

Do as You're Told: Compliance

Organizations that are premised on compliance expect the individual willingly to play a bounded, subordinate role for the good of the larger enterprise. One is supposed to be dedicated to the organization in the same way that certain production processes are "dedicated" to a particular product—to the exclusion of anything else.

Compliance-based organizations tend to emphasize the obligations of subordinates to higher-ups. The ideal profile of an employee likely matches that of Lt. Col. Oliver North as depicted in *The Wall Street Journal* during President Reagan's Iranscam flap. Col. North "lived by the chain of command and strove to please his superiors. . . . [He was] a man who throughout his life has nurtured a series of close relationships with male authority figures, including athletics coaches and military bosses. To many of these men, Oliver North—college boxing champion, war hero, and fast-track Marine officer—was the perfect surrogate son."[48]

Work Together: Collaboration

Where collaboration is the guiding organizational expectation, we find people continually looking out for others, searching for new ways to contribute by metaphorically making that extra pass. There may be no better example than 3M, where solutions are as likely to drive the search for problems as the other way around—just because corporate scientists are convinced "that somewhere in 3M someone will be able to use almost anything."[49] Back-and-forth exchanges among specialists from different disciplines are the norm.

A similar dynamic prevails at Nucor. Says maintenance technician Rod Zilles, "When something goes down, people ask me how they can help. Nobody sits around. Every minute you are down, it's like dollars out of your back pocket. So everybody really hustles."[50]

Individual Expectation

The Brass Ring: Opportunity

Each organizational expectation has its individual quid pro quo. If the organization counts on its employees to be self-reliant, then the latter are going to expect the organization to provide them with significant opportunities for development and advancement. People who are expected to stand on their own two feet and take risks are unlikely to be very patient with a slow-trajectory career path that does not pay off commensurately. This seems to be the case with many "fast-track" MBAs. The president of one major manufacturer has stated categorically: "MBAs are not team players."[51]

Here Today, Here Tomorrow: Security

The flip side of compliance is security. For decades people have signed up and saluted, with the implicit understanding that their employment contract was forever. Needless to say, the last few years have jolted all this. It has been estimated that in the period 1983 through 1988, as many as 1.5 million middle- and upper-level managers will have been displaced from major corporations as a result of cutbacks, takeovers, mergers, and business failures.[52]

Loyalty to the employee is a tougher act to pull off now than in the past. Still, certain companies remain committed to it. One of the best indexes of commitment is an employment security policy; Delta Air Lines, Federal Express, Herman Miller, IBM, and Nucor are some of the firms that practice such a policy. Yet even the best intentions may be dashed, as employees at People Express and Bank of America—companies that also had employment security policies—so painfully learned.

A Sense of Belonging: Community

If the organization expects collaboration among employees, employees will likely expect the organization to foster a sense of community. A key aspect of this is an egalitarian atmosphere in which status symbols that separate employees into different classes are minimized.

Size, too, is important. Although there may be no one maximum number of employees that is too many for a single facility, a sense of human scale does suggest limits. A livable size helps people see how their work fits in with that of other units and with the company as a whole. It also reinforces a feeling of social support at work because it allows people to get to know each other. In fact, one of the most effective ways to stimulate a sense of community is to encourage people to eat or have a drink together. It is doubtful that any group will ever knit if it does not share a coffee pot or regularly break bread together.

At the level of the facility—that is, the office, plant, building, or mill—the equivalent of a shared meal is a "town meeting" or other event that involves everybody. From time to time the whole needs to see itself as one. In sum, a spirit of community is unlikely to develop unless people both eat together and meet together.

Cultural Bias

My Way: Diversity

Every company, and every unit within it, has a distinctive culture that can be characterized as a mix of diversity, uniformity, and complementarity. An organization that is biased toward diversity cherishes differences in thought and behavior. Top universities obviously fit this pattern. But so do certain corporations. Ed Carlson, former CEO of United Airlines, took pains to hire managers of different ages and from different backgrounds—some with substantial airline experience and others with none at all. He believed that the richness of perspectives easily justified this practice.

Cray Research's creed nicely sums up a bias for diversity:

Because the individual is key at Cray, there is a real diversity in the view of what Cray Research really is. In fact, Cray Research is many things to many people. The consistency comes in providing those diverse people with the opportunity to fulfill themselves and experience achievement. The creativity, then, that emerges from the company comes from the many ideas of the individuals who are here. And that is the real strength of Cray Research.[53]

The Company Way: Uniformity

Uniformity is the byword at companies such as ITT and Arthur Andersen. At ITT, chairman Rand Araskog assembled what *The Wall Street Journal* described as "a management team fashioned, to an unusual degree, in his own image."[54] Araskog initiated a requirement that his subordinates submit biweekly reports to him and allow him to scrutinize their monthly calendars. Replied senior vice-president Robert J. Braverman, "If I were concerned about being by myself and not having someone watch what I do, I would have left ITT long ago."

Arthur Andersen's emphasis on uniformity is revealed by its training center, which has been compared to Marine boot camp. The firm justifies this unit by noting that its recruits are serious, no-frills types: "Arthur Andersen places a premium on consistency and says the huge, busy center turns out 800 new accountants per class, all able to do everything exactly the same way—'the Arthur Andersen way.'"[55]

Our Way: Complementarity

A bias for complementarity recognizes the mutual importance of organizational resources—that any individual or unit may have a legitimate claim on the capacities of another individual or unit. This bias is found at such companies as 3M and Hewlett-Packard. Hewlett-Packard has long had a tradition in which people are expected to move fluidly among several teams as technical needs and product life cycles dictate. More recently, the same dynamic of volunteering complementary skills has taken place across divisions, just as it has at such other technically-oriented firms as Honeywell and NEC.

One of the best examples of inter-unit complementarity that I know of involved two business units, in separate divisions, of James River Corporation: James River Graphics and James River–Otis. In a letter acknowledging the presentation of its "Partners-in-Progress" award to Otis, Graphics' technical manager Rick Taylor listed five concrete examples of Otis's contributions to Graphics. He then went on to say the following:

> For all that we have accomplished, we have a great deal more to look forward to. I believe we have the vision to develop a quality information system which will help to further improve product consistency and aid in design improvements. I believe that together we can develop a new [product] which will be of such value to the end-user that we will establish James River as the most-preferred worldwide supplier. I believe that successful completion of our [product] strategy will serve as an example to the rest of the Corporation as to how decentralized, autonomous business units can work together for the good of the Corporation.

You have now reviewed in detail all 10 dimensions of the Teamwork Profile. The next step is to use this framework in characterizing your own organization. Chapter 4 lays out the process. Chapter 5 will then explain how to articulate organizational mission, and show how this statement matches up with design. Succeeding chapters will address change: visualizing the organization the way you want it to be, and making the necessary commitments to get there.

Chapter Four

Assessing Organizational Design

In a long-running magazine advertisement John W. Teets, chairman of Greyhound Corporation, proclaims that "management's job is to see the company not as it is . . . but as it can become." Such sentiment reflects the popularity of visions and "visioning" of late. The intent of Teets's statement, no doubt, is to make the contrast between present and future. But taken literally, this point of view can be problematic: It is difficult—if not impossible—to become what you want to be if you don't know what you are.

I believe that management has three challenges: (1) to see the company as it is, (2) to see it as it should be, and (3) to determine what it will be. The "willed" organization will almost always be a blend of what is and what, ideally, should be.

Seeing the company as it is means having a clear picture of both organizational design and mission. The mission of any organization, regardless of size, is its purpose, its raison d'être. The question should always be, To what ends is teamwork directed? Hence, the management team should seriously think through both the nature of the current organization and its actual mission. Which activity should be undertaken first? My own preference is to lay out organizational design up front, for two reasons. First, this exercise is more likely to ground deliberations in concrete matters that everyone can grasp; that is, organizational design is less ethereal than mission and therefore can provide a more "real" base on which to build. Such concreteness is especially advantageous where lines of business are blurred, as is often the case with financial services and computers/communications, for example.[1] Second, starting with organizational design gives people a systematic framework and vocabulary that they can use over and over in the future. Indeed, it is a framework that can be immediately helpful in defining current mission.

The key point, however, is not whether organizational design or mission comes first; it is rather that these issues should be considered in tandem. Neither can be completed without reference to the other.

ORGANIZATIONAL DESIGN

Two basic instruments are used. With the first, the *Teamwork Profile* (Figure 4.1), the task is to define the most accurate blend of autonomy, control, and cooperation for each dimension by spreading five (5) points across the three columns.

The second instrument, the *Teamwork Triangle* (Figure 4.2), is a graphic device for summarizing and communicating the patterns identified in the Teamwork Profile.

The Triangle is made up of 10 geometrical shapes: three white trapezoids, three white triangles, and four shaded triangles. The white shapes represent "viable" organizational designs; the shaded shapes, "vulnerable" designs—running the risk of either overdoing a particular form of teamwork (the corners) or having insufficient teamwork priorities (the center triangle).[2]

THE ASSESSMENT PROCESS

The initial diagnosis is best carried out by a management team of 4 to 12 people (5 to 8 is optimal). Here's how to do it:

(1) Review the 10 dimensions of the Teamwork Profile, which were spelled out in Chapter 3. Make sure everyone is clear about the meaning of each dimension.

Figure 4.1. Teamwork Profile

	AUTONOMY (Baseball)	CONTROL (Football)	COOPERATION (Basketball)

ORGANIZATIONAL STRATEGY

	AUTONOMY (Baseball)	CONTROL (Football)	COOPERATION (Basketball)
• Distinctive competence (What organizational competencies separate us from our competition?)	Adding value through star performers ( )	Reducing costs and/or complexity through global coordination ( )	Innovating by combining resources in novel ways ( )
• Developmental pattern (How do we pursue development/ renewal/ growth?)	From the outside ( )	From within ( )	In concert with others ( )

ORGANIZATIONAL STRUCTURE

	AUTONOMY (Baseball)	CONTROL (Football)	COOPERATION (Basketball)
• Coordinating mechanism (How do we manage interdependence?)	Design of free-standing roles/units ( )	Hierarchical planning and administration ( )	Mutual adjustment ( )
• Decision system (Who is involved in decision-making, when, and in what ways?)	Decentralized ( )	Centralized ( )	Shared ( )
• Information system (Who has access to the information necessary to make decisions?)	Locally controlled ( )	Globally controlled ( )	Distributed ( )

Figure 4.1. (Continued)

	AUTONOMY (Baseball)		CONTROL (Football)		COOPERATION (Basketball)	
• Reward system (What behaviors are reinforced financially and nonfinancially?)	Individualistic	( )	Hierarchic	( )	Mutualistic	( )
• Effect of physical configuration (What human interaction does our physical design encourage?)	Independent action	( )	Programmed interaction	( )	Spontaneous interaction	( )

ORGANIZATIONAL STYLE

• Organizational expectation (What does the organization expect from its people?)	Self-reliance	( )	Compliance	( )	Collaboration	( )
• Individual expectation (What do people expect from their organization?)	Opportunity	( )	Security	( )	Community	( )
• Cultural bias (What is our overriding social value?)	Diversity	( )	Uniformity	( )	Complementarity	( )

TOTALS:		( )		( )		( )

Figure 4.2. Teamwork Triangle

COOPERATION
(Basketball)

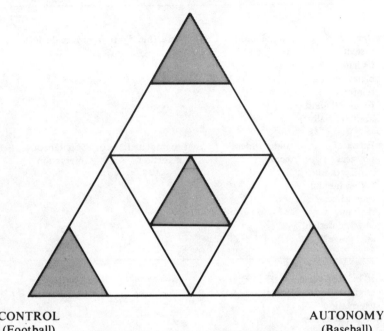

CONTROL
(Football)

AUTONOMY
(Baseball)

(2) Agree on your unit of analysis. Is it the whole company? A particular division? A plant or an office?
A department? In general, the initial unit of analysis
should be the largest organizational unit represented
by the team. Thus, if your team consists of the CEO
or COO and people reporting directly to him or her,
the unit of analysis should be the whole company; if
the team is made up of a divisional vice president/
general manager and the next two levels of management, then the unit should be the division as a whole;
and so on.

(3) *Individually* complete the Teamwork Profile, distributing five points across each dimension, to describe the current organization as you actually see it—good or bad. Then add up the three columns; altogether they should total 50 (10 dimensions × five points), as in the example below (Figure 4.3).

(4) Convert your Teamwork Profile totals into a mark on the Teamwork Triangle by applying judgment to the following guidelines. If all three column totals are virtually equal (e.g., 16–16–18), then mark the shaded center triangle. If one column is dominant (e.g., 38–8–4), then mark the appropriate shaded corner. If two columns are dominant (e.g., 20–10–20), then mark the appropriate small white triangle. If none of the above applies—so that there are significant differences between your highest, middle, and lowest totals (e.g., 16–26–8)—then mark the appropriate trapezoid.

These guidelines, which are summarized in Figure 4.4, are purposely loose.

No one formula is correct for all organizations. What is an excessive degree of autonomy (or control or cooperation) in one context may be perfectly reasonable in another. And it may make sense to weight some dimensions more heavily than others. I should add that the precise location inside the shape is immaterial; this would represent a finer measurement than is necessary. Figure 4.5 converts the numbers from Figure 4.3 onto the Teamwork Triangle.

(5) Combine everyone's marks on the Teamwork Triangle into a summary Triangle. This gives the team a clear picture of the range of individual impressions.

Figure 4.3. Sample Teamwork Profile

	AUTONOMY (Baseball)		CONTROL (Football)		COOPERATION (Basketball)	

ORGANIZATIONAL STRATEGY

	AUTONOMY (Baseball)		CONTROL (Football)		COOPERATION (Basketball)	
• Distinctive competence (What organizational competencies separate us from our competition?)	Adding value through star performers	(1)	Reducing costs and/or complexity through global coordination	(3)	Innovating by combining resources in novel ways	(1)
• Developmental pattern (How do we pursue development/ renewal/ growth?)	From the outside	(0)	From within	(5)	In concert with others	(0)

ORGANIZATIONAL STRUCTURE

	AUTONOMY (Baseball)		CONTROL (Football)		COOPERATION (Basketball)	
• Coordinating mechanism (How do we manage interdependence?)	Design of free-standing roles/units	(3)	Hierarchical planning and administration	(2)	Mutual adjustment	(0)
• Decision system (Who is involved in decision-making, when, and in what ways?)	Decentralized	(2)	Centralized	(2)	Shared	(1)
• Information system (Who has access to the information necessary to make decisions?)	Locally controlled	(1)	Globally controlled	(3)	Distributed	(1)

Figure 4.3. (Continued)

	AUTONOMY (Baseball)		CONTROL (Football)		COOPERATION (Basketball)	
• Reward system (What behaviors are reinforced financially and nonfinancially?)	Individualistic	(1)	Hierarchic	(4)	Mutualistic	(0)
• Effect of physical configuration (What human interaction does our physical design encourage?)	Independent action	(5)	Programmed interaction	(0)	Spontaneous interaction	(0)

ORGANIZATIONAL STYLE

• Organizational expectation (What does the organization expect from its people?)	Self-reliance	(2)	Compliance	(1)	Collaboration	(2)
• Individual expectation (What do people expect from their organization?)	Opportunity	(1)	Security	(3)	Community	(1)
• Cultural bias (What is our overriding social value?)	Diversity	(0)	Uniformity	(3)	Complementarity	(2)

TOTALS:		(16)		(26)		(8)

Figure 4.4. Converting Scores to the Teamwork Triangle

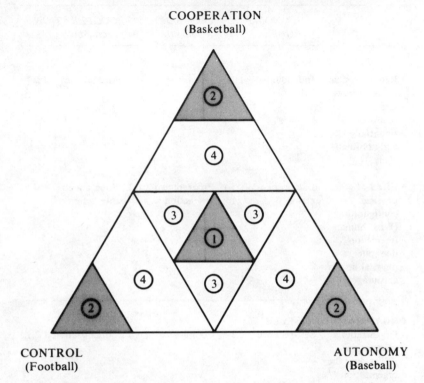

COOPERATION
(Basketball)

CONTROL
(Football)

AUTONOMY
(Baseball)

Legend:

① All three column totals virtually equal

② One column dominant

③ Two columns dominant

④ None of the above (significant differences between highest, middle, and lowest totals)

Figure 4.6 shows a sample distribution for a team of eight managers.

(6) *As a team*, work your way through the Profile, one dimension at a time, comparing perceptions. Reach

Figure 4.5. Figure 4.3 Converted to Teamwork Triangle

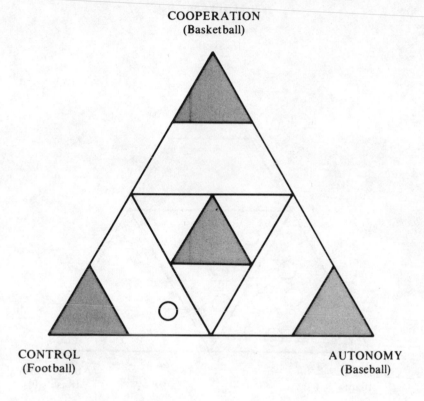

COOPERATION
(Basketball)

CONTROL
(Football)

AUTONOMY
(Baseball)

agreement on how to distribute five points across each dimension. After you have completed the Profile, add up the three columns, which should total 50.

(7) Convert your team's Teamwork Profile totals into a mark on the Teamwork Triangle, using the guidelines provided by Figure 4.4.

The process outlined above may or may not be sufficient for accurately describing the current design—that determination rests with your team. One obvious shortcoming is the

**Figure 4.6. Sample Distribution of Team Members'
Individual Impressions**

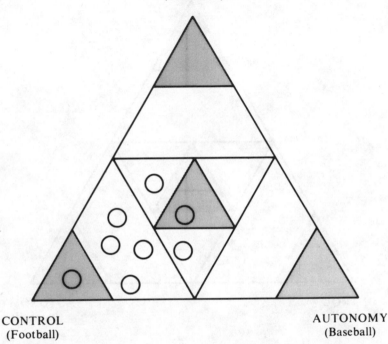

COOPERATION
(Basketball)

CONTROL
(Football)

AUTONOMY
(Baseball)

limited point of view that is expressed. This exercise produces the collective opinion of a small group—the management team—about a much larger whole.

Another difficulty with the group assessment process is also a potential advantage: the likelihood that different team members have different frames of reference. In the course of discussion, people should make explicit the referents that they used in completing the Teamwork Profile (and that they probably use implicitly day to day). Whenever we make statements about our organization, it is always with certain other organizations in mind—however subconsciously—as bases for comparison. No organization exists within a mental vacuum. If a team member believes that his or her firm's reward structure is "individualistic," the relevant question is, "Compared to what?" Thus, Ross Perot's EDS may have exuded autonomy in relation to General Motors, but less so when compared to Cray Research.

In sum, by making known their bases for comparison, all team members gain a better understanding of where everyone is coming from—a necessary preliminary step to achieving a shared team identity. It is an exercise whose practical value will become especially apparent when the team articulates its organizational mission (Chapter 5). For then the issue of appropriate model organizations—to whom do we compare ourselves?—is central.

REDUCING SUBJECTIVITY

There are three ways to reduce the subjectivity of the group assessment procedure: (1) sampling of organizational perceptions; (2) off-line assessment—that is, outside the team-meeting setting—in which non-team members play a major role (team members may or may not be directly involved); and (3) analysis by the team itself during extended meetings. These tacks are complementary and can be undertaken in parallel.

Sampling of Organizational Perceptions

Your team can solicit impressions from throughout the company by asking various employees to complete the Teamwork Profile for the organization as a whole, and then share their perceptions. It may be revealing to cluster employees in order to determine if differences are important. For instance, individuals might be grouped by some mix of hierarchical level, job responsibility or type, unit (division, location, department, function), subculture, tenure, and so on. Depending on time and other resource constraints, it may be worthwhile to have an internal or external consultant use the Teamwork Profile in group interviews.

In addition to providing valuable information that can fill in your team's blind spots, this approach begins to develop widespread commitment to organizational analysis and change. People like to feel a part of things. Asking for their impressions can be an important way to include them early in the process.

Off-Line Assessment

Most dimensions making up organizational strategy and organizational structure (see Figure 4.1) lend themselves to objective, off-line analysis. *Distinctive competence*—the organization's competitive edge—may best be determined by querying customers, internal as well as external. Some firms routinely use consultants to learn customers' opinions about their performance. Often the results are unexpected. One organization that was convinced its competitive strength lay in the quality of its professional staff was surprised to learn that many of its customers—and potential customers—viewed it as a cost-driven operation in which staff qualifications were of secondary importance.

Developmental pattern can refer to a host of processes—product/market growth, technological know-how, and recruitment/promotional practices, among other things. Once your team is clear about which patterns are most relevant, it can commission an historical analysis that shows what actual steps the organization has taken over time. If desired, this analysis can identify developmental stages that highlight particular tendencies.

For instance, the focus might be on reconstructing the firm's technical skill base over the last five years. A study could reveal the extent to which skills were (1) purchased from the outside (in the form of new hires and/or acquired companies), (2) generated in-house, or (3) developed in collaboration with other organizations (or other units within the corporation).

The most direct way to determine *coordinating mechanism* is to ask managers from the major organizational units to characterize the dominant form of interdependence—pooled, sequential, or reciprocal—among them. Their responses can be visually summarized by drawing arrows horizontally, between interacting units, on an organization chart.

Unfortunately, organization charts do not specify either a company's *decision system* or its *information system*. They may tell us who reports to whom, and who is at what level, but they reveal little about how decisions actually get made or where information flows. Some companies (like the one cited in Chapter 2) have analyzed their decision-making structure in terms of centralization and decentralization: which decisions are made at headquarters, which are made at operating units, and which are a combination? While such breakdowns typically ignore shared decision-making—within and between facilities, divisions, functions, and so on—they can still be helpful. (Corporate failure to recognize shared decision-making may or may not signal a relative absence of this pattern throughout the organization. It certainly suggests as much.)

Another obvious resource for the decision system is any policy manual that spells out, for instance, dollar expenditure authorities by job title or hierarchical position. Likewise, a protocol held by management information systems/data processing that indicates who is to receive what information can help to flesh out the information system. As an alternative or a supplement, it may be worthwhile to verify which individuals/units are connected—whether electronically, through routine reports, or in other ways.

An organization's *reward system* refers to both financial and nonfinancial rewards. It should be a relatively easy matter to put together figures that describe the pay system. Comparative information, such as that provided by trade association or industry-wide surveys, can supply perspective. With respect to status symbols, recognition programs, and other nonfinancial rewards, consultants and other outside observers can be a source of relatively unbiased information.

To gauge the *effect of physical configuration*, your team may either obtain a diagram of the current layout or charter a study that identifies interaction patterns among locations, units, or individuals. In some cases, of course—like the old-fashioned assembly line—all one need do is take a look at the setting, or a drawing or photo of it, to figure out the kind and degree of interaction that it promotes.

One observation here. My experience is that many companies tend to underestimate the isolating effects of distance, especially vertical distance. In one firm with which I am familiar, people in the same building but three floors apart interact informally on the job about as much as others in the same corporation who are three thousand (horizontal) miles apart. "We just never see each other" is the simple explanation. I doubt that this case is unusual.

The elements of organizational style—*organizational expectation*, *individual expectation*, and *cultural bias*—are all considerably softer and more elusive than those grouped under organizational strategy and structure. Archival and other "hard" evidence is more difficult to come by. Your team may therefore authorize a survey in which people throughout the organization share their perceptions anonymously. (Alternatively, the organizational sampling referred to above can be used to provide this information.)

Off-line analysis, like organizational sampling, has the advantage of transcending the boundary of the small group. In each case people outside your team, and sometimes outside the organization, provide important vantages; they serve as an antidote to tendencies toward team implosion or "groupthink." The primary drawbacks are time and cost. The anticipated payback may simply not justify the effort. Of course, a compromise is to sponsor analysis only on certain dimensions.

Self-Analysis

Systematic analysis by your team itself has much to recommend it. Not the least of its strengths is the bonding among team members that it stimulates. The more a group of people jointly seek to make sense of the organization they lead, the more unified they will become. At the same time, this process of inquiry will generate creative tension toward improving the organization. In all, considerable *team-building* is a natural by-product of organizational diagnosis.

The two areas that in my experience most lend themselves to systematic self-analysis are (1) the decision system and (2) the elements of organizational style: organizational expectation, individual expectation, and cultural bias. These areas can be explored by two respective techniques: decision analysis and norm specification.

Decision Analysis

Who is involved in decision-making, when, and in what ways? These are the questions that decision analysis addresses. A variation on a technique called "responsibility charting,"[3] decision analysis enables your team to understand the nature of the organization's overall decision system—to what extent it is decentralized, centralized, and shared.

There are three ways to make a decision, which correspond to the three types of decision system: (1) to delegate (decentralized system), (2) to mandate (centralized), and (3) to collaborate (shared). When a manager delegates, he or she transfers decision-making authority to a subordinate. When he mandates a decision, a manager decides unilaterally. When a manager collaborates, he enters into a joint decision-making process with others.

Collaboration typically takes one of two forms. Under the first form, consultation, a manager solicits input from subordinates (and/or peers) before making a decision, but retains go/no-go authority. Under the second form, consensus, manager and subordinates jointly shape the decision or solution or course of action. Consensus is thus a more complex process than consultation. Minimally, consensus means that: (1) everyone on the team has had input (or the opportunity to provide input) prior to the decision point, and (2) everyone is willing to go along with the team's decision—even though this decision may not be everyone's first choice (thus, consensus does not necessarily imply unanimity).

The three basic decision-making modes are summarized in Table 4.1.

In fact, there are two additional varieties of "collaborative" decision-making: compromise and vote. Both have the advantage of speed (like mandate) and are often used to sup-

Table 4.1   MODES OF DECISION-MAKING

	DEFINITION	*STRENGTHS*	*WEAKNESSES*
1. Delegate	Subordinates decide (within boundaries set by manager)	Authority moved close to action; subordinates "own" decision; delegator's time freed up	Can be risky because assumes subordinate competence; may ignore interdependencies among subordinates
2. Mandate	Manager decides unilaterally	Global perspective; ease of reaching decision	Possible insensitivity to local conditions; implementation difficult because implementers do not own decision
3. Collaborate a. Consult	Manager decides after consultation with subordinates	Multiple resources brought to bear; implementers have some decision ownership	Somewhat time-consuming decision process
b. Achieve consensus	Manager and subordinates jointly decide	Multiple resources brought to bear; implementers own decision	Time-consuming, even frustrating decision process

plement a consensual process. But each has a serious liability as a general method, so both modes are usually excluded from the decision analysis: Compromise tends to restrict the consideration of options—one settles for the average of A and B, rather than considering C, D, E, and so on. As a result, a less than high-quality alternative may be selected. Voting tends to polarize a group into pro and con, majority and minority, *winners and losers*—thereby provoking a divisiveness that is contrary to team spirit.

By mapping patterns of delegating, mandating, and collaborating, your team can clarify the kind of decision system by which the organization operates. The first step is to arrive at a decision vocabulary. A home-grown language, using words that have a shared meaning for all team members, is perfectly acceptable. A key consideration, however, should be simplicity. I have found that a three-word vocabulary, abbreviated below, can be quite effective:[4]

D: Decision-making authority; having go/no-go authority;

C: Consulting input; having influence on the decision/decision-maker;

I: Informational involvement; being informed that a decision is about to be made or has been made.

Consulting input (C) covers a lot of ground. At one extreme, a person with this designation may have only superficial influence on a decision; at the other extreme, he or she may be the de facto decision-maker—as is often the case when one is asked to screen a multitude of alternatives (e.g., the resumés of job applicants) and then make a recommendation to the "official" decision-maker. This vagueness is intentional. It adds to the flexibility of the vocabulary by acknowledging a wide range of behaviors between final authority and no authority. And the reality for most, if not all, organizations is that the strength of consulting input for any given decision area will vary with the particular situation and the needs at that time; hence, some maneuvering room is essential. I should add, however, that some teams find it useful to distinguish strong consulting input from weak by using capital and lower-case *c*'s.

After agreeing on a vocabulary, the next step is to generate a set of the major decisions/decision areas with which the organization is concerned. For instance, the senior management team of an industrial products division of a major corporation developed the following initial list:

- Sales policies
- Product line issues
- Inventory levels
- Organizational/personnel issues
- Interaction among divisional facilities
- Interaction between division and other corporate units
- Strategic direction and yardsticks
- Planning

The next step is to "explode" these decision areas into a larger number of narrower decisions. A decision matrix is then created by listing decisions along one axis (typically the left side of a flip chart) and players—that is, organizational members (or units)—along the other axis (the top of the flip chart). The analytical task is to review each decision to clarify who is involved, at what point, and how. The industrial products division cited above, for example, completed the following (abridged) matrix for the first category it identified, Sales policies (Figure 4.7). (Roles have been simplified and decision patterns revised for illustrative purposes.)

Figure 4.7 conveys a sense of the complexity that can be mapped by decision analysis. The streamlined "organization" consists of just two levels—the divisional general manager and his three direct reports—but a variety of patterns can be specified. Decision #7 is an example of a combination pattern. The general manager has delegated this decision to his staff planner, who is expected to consult with both sales vice presidents and the GM before reaching a decision.

After completing decision analysis, your team can review dominant patterns in order to characterize the organization's decision system in terms of decentralization/centralization/sharing. If Figure 4.7 were representative, for example, and no issues of decision weighting needed to be dealt with, then the team could consider the current system to be primarily a decentralized/shared (autonomy/cooperation) blend.

Norm Specification

A norm is a tacit rule of behavior, a usually-unwritten understanding of what is right and what is wrong. Every social system—from the family to the nation—has a distinctive set of norms, or behavioral ground rules. By making explicit the norms by which the organization operates, your team can gain considerable insight into stylistic patterns.[5]

As an organizing framework to stimulate thinking about norms, I have often used a mnemonic based on the letter "t": taboos, traditions, trappings, turf, tempo, technology, trust, and teamwork. Representative norms that reflect autonomy, control, and cooperation, respectively, are shown in Table 4.2.

Figure 4.7. Sample Decision Matrix

PLAYERS: / DECISIONS:	Div GM	VP Sales, U.S.	VP Sales, Int'l	Staff Plan-ner	(Type of decision process)
1. Determine what consti-tutes a major account	D	I	I	I	(mandate)
2. Develop pricing policy	D	D	D		(collaborate/ consensus)
3. Implement pricing policy		Ⓓ	Ⓓ		(delegate)*
4. Authorize changes to pricing policy	D	D	D		(collaborate/ consensus)
5. Prepare freight schedule	I	I	I	D	(delegate)
6. Establish returns and allowances terms	D	C	C		(collaborate/ consulting)
7. Design incen-tive pay struc-ture	C	C	C	D	(delegate and collaborate/ consulting)
8. Assess/revise distribution system	I	(Ⓓ)	(Ⓓ)		(delegate)**

Legend: D: Decision-making authority
C: Consulting input
I: Informational involvement

*A circle D [Ⓓ] indicates that the individuals to whom decision-making au-thority has been delegated need not interact; each can make his or her own decision independently of the other(s).

**A broken-circle D [(Ⓓ)] indicates that the individuals to whom authority has been delegated sometimes need to interact, and at other times do not; it is up to each of these individuals to know when to act jointly and when to act independently.

Table 4.2   AN ORGANIZING FRAMEWORK
FOR SPECIFYING NORMS

	AUTONOMY	*CONTROL*	*COOPERATION*
TABOOS	Not taking initiative	Doing one's own thing	Withholding help
TRADITIONS	Celebrating freedom	Celebrating continuity	Celebrating flexibility
TRAPPINGS	Horizontal differentiation of people	Vertical differentiation of people	Integration of people
TURF	Property of each individual	Property of the organization	Property of everyone
TEMPO	Civilized	Regimented	Electric
TECHNOLOGY	To enhance individual performance	To constrain/ replace people	To enhance group performance
TRUST	In each individual's capacity	In the wisdom of management	In group processes
TEAMWORK	Situational	Scripted	Shared

The above framework is most meaningful when people can cite concrete evidence—episodes, incidents, events—in support of the words. It is then a relatively easy matter to go from the organizing framework to a more precise statement of norms that matches the three components of organizational style. But the framework is optional. Some teams prefer to work without it. In either case, the object is to articulate characteristics of organizational style such as those illustrated in Table 4.3.

Table 4.3 CLARIFYING ASPECTS OF ORGANIZATIONAL STYLE

	SELF-RELIANCE	LOYALTY	COLLABOR-ATION
ORGANIZA-TIONAL EXPECTATION	Hire the best people and leave them alone	Never say anything negative about the company to an outsider	Spread the credit
	You've got to be a self-starter to survive	We want people who are in it for the long haul	Build consensus

	OPPORTUNITY	SECURITY	COMMUNITY
INDIVIDUAL EXPECTATION	Put out and you'll make out	Keep your nose clean and you're set for life	We are family
	Everybody's a profit center here	Job security is a moral obligation	This place cares about your whole life, not just the part on company time

	DIVERSITY	UNIFORMITY	COMPLEMEN-TARITY
CULTURAL BIAS	Creativity comes from different points of view	Do it by the book	No one is so smart that he can figure out everything by himself
	Each division has a unique culture and we like that	We present one face to the customer, regardless of which part of the company is involved	Our strength is the synergy we get by involving all of the functions at the same time

CONCLUDING COMMENTS

This chapter has shown how you can characterize teamwork in your company or in any unit of it. The simplest method is for the management team to complete the Teamwork Profile—first individually and next as a group—and then transfer this information onto the Teamwork Triangle.

Three more rigorous methods were outlined: (1) sampling perceptions of others in the organization: (2) systematically assessing the organization "off-line," that is, outside of the management-team process; and (3) "self-analysis," a more exhaustive diagnosis by the management team itself.

Any mix of these methods is workable. The important criteria are your needs, resources, and inclination. I am not a believer in detail for detail's sake. Accordingly, my usual recommendation to management teams is to put less effort into assessing what is, and more into determining what should be and what will be. I still believe, however, that understanding one's current state is prerequisite to moving towards a desired state.

With that thought in mind, the management team needs to be clear about actual organizational mission—whether explicit or implicit—before articulating what it desires. The elements of mission, and how they relate to organizational design, are the subject of Chapter 5.

Chapter Five

Articulating Mission

Articulating your organization's mission—its reason for existence—represents a broadening of team design. Mission cannot be defined as a mix of three models in the same way that organizational design can. Yet every mission statement should include three basic categories: character, customers, and capabilities.

COMPONENTS OF MISSION

Character

Your organization's character is its personality, its identity. Character is defined by deeply shared values and aspirations that distinguish the organization from all others. Your company's character is what makes it special—indeed, unique. Character denotes a distinctive vision and set of priorities; it refers both to the internal organization and to the external contributions to which the organization is committed.

In making character explicit, it is important to home in on noneconomic (as well as economic) principles that are most meaningful. Representative concerns addressed by companies with which I have worked are:

- Change

- Cooperation

- Creativity

- Delegation

- Employment continuity

- Environment

- Ethics

- Health

- Honesty

- Human development

- Information-sharing

- Integrity

- Product quality

- Profitability

- Relationships

- Risk-taking

- Safety

- Social responsibility

- Technological leadership

Such principles should be articulated in relation to the firm's constituencies or stakeholders, and should express perceived obligations to each. Typical stakeholders include, in addition to the familiar stockholders: customers, suppliers, employees, unions/employee associations, the local community, the general public, and regulatory agencies. Some examples of corporate responses:

CUSTOMER/VENDOR RELATIONSHIPS. We strive for long-term, close business relationships with **customers** and **key vendors**. This is critical to establishing clear objectives, optimizing total system performance, and understanding evolving technical and market trends. We will build these relationships on openness and mutual trust while recognizing and respecting each other's proprietary needs. [James River Graphics]

EMPLOYEES. [Our objective is] to offer participation in ADP's success in which . . . [employees] play an important role . . . by offering challenges, opportunities for creativity, rewards, security, personal skills development, and performance feedback. Our rewards should include competitive wages, above-average opportunities for promotions, supplemental gain from ADP's stock participation plans, and psychic income from accomplishment in an informal, apolitical, fast-paced environment. [Automatic Data Processing, Inc.]

COMMUNITY. We are responsible to the communities in which we live and work and to the world community as well. We must be good citizens—support good works and charities and bear our fair share of taxes. We must encourage civic improvements and better health and education. We must maintain in good order the property we are privileged to use, protecting the environment and natural resources. [Johnson & Johnson]

Customers

If "character" describes your organization's essential nature, *what* it stands for, then "customers" is shorthand for *whom* it serves, and with what products and/or services. In other words, what is your product/market domain? Product/market domain is what many managers implicitly have in mind when they talk about this or that "game," in which their own or other companies are players.

In defining your domain, two essentials are segmentation and coherence. Customer segmentation pinpoints whom you will serve. Typical dimensions to consider are:

- Class of customer (retail, commercial, industrial, governmental, etc.)
- Geography (local, regional, national, international, etc.)

- Demographics (age, sex, income, education, occupation, etc.)

- Psychographics (aspirations, fears, tolerance for uncertainty, etc.)

Customer segmentation differentiates your customers or clients from all others. A necessary complement to this process is integrative: ensuring product/market coherence.

A major reason 3M can succeed with a market basket of more than 50,000 products is the common bonding and coating technology that underlies these products. 3M in this respect illustrates the intersection of the "customers" and "capabilities" aspects of mission. And indeed, common technology helps define 3M's character, just as does the firm's commitment to sharing ideas all across the company (an example of the overlap between character and capabilities).

Several recent studies generalize the importance of product/market coherence. For example, analyses of both large, diversified corporations[1] and high-growth, midsize companies[2] have found that as a rule, diversification into related products/markets has been more successful than unrelated diversification.

Capabilities

Your organization's capabilities are the ways that it meets customer needs. This is the *how* dimension—how your company competes within a given product/market realm. To clarify organizational capabilities, some measure of priority must be assigned to such diverse criteria as:

- Quality/durability/functionality/prestige

- Cost/consistency

- Service/flexibility/customer responsiveness/breadth of product line

- Innovation/creativity/novelty/technology

Sometimes companies focus on a single, guiding criterion. In its 1985 annual report, for instance, American Express claims that "Our strategy depends first and foremost on un-excelled service to customers. Superior service has, for many years, been the essence of American Express: *the* factor that has distinguished us from the competition."

In other cases, multiple criteria are identified. Thus CIGNA Corporation, in its 1985 annual report, points to four related capabilities that it feels differentiate the firm from its competitors:

" . . . our employees' commitment to service, the breadth of our product and service portfolio, the global scope of our operations, and the development and use of new technology. We are convinced that the continued development of these four distinguishing marketplace strengths will enhance CIGNA's abilities to provide high-quality and cost-effective service that will make it attractive for customers to maintain existing business with us and to purchase additional products and services from us."

Both the American Express and CIGNA statements are examples of placing value-addition—chiefly in the form of high-quality service—ahead of cost-reduction. But in neither case is cost-*competitiveness* irrelevant; minimizing cost is simply not the top priority.

Contrast this perspective with that of Green Bay, Wisconsin-based Fort Howard Paper Co., whose chairman and CEO, Paul J. Schierl, has been likened to another Green Bay notable, former Packers' head coach Vince Lombardi. Says Schierl:

> In our industry, success comes from either having a unique competitive advantage with the products sold or from being able to produce the products at a lower cost than anyone else. Because tissue and cups are basically commodity-type products—that is, little difference in product that would command a price premium—we have to be the low cost producer in our industry. And we consistently strive to achieve and maintain that low cost producer status.[3]

CHARACTER, CUSTOMERS, AND CAPABILITIES IN PERSPECTIVE

The three categories just described are no more exhaustive than they are exclusive. In fact, most thoughtful mission statements will combine these and possibly other categories into a composite declaration. The value of the three categories is that they provide a minimum framework for analysis; every organization should be clear about what it is, whom it serves, and how.

Character and capabilities frequently overlap, as suggested by some recent corporate slogans and pledges:

- "We don't cut corners" (quality)—Hartmann
- "We run the tightest ship in the shipping business" (cost/delivery)—UPS

- "Over 150 years of progress and stability" (reliability)— Allendale Insurance

- "Delta is ready when you are" (service)—Delta Airlines

- "A generation ahead" (technical innovation)—Data General

- "One great idea after another" (new-product development)—Lotus Development Corp.

- "Everybody is somebody at Dean Witter" (customer responsiveness)—Dean Witter

- "Together, we can find the answers" (collaboration)— Honeywell

Perhaps one test of the degree to which such language actually mirrors organizational character is its life span: the longer that words remain in good currency, the more likely it is that they do express fundamental character. But the words themselves are less important than the pattern of values that is conveyed; an organization may vary its motto over time yet still express the same core meaning.

When a company institutionalizes a guarantee—such as Federal Express's with respect to overnight delivery or Holiday Inns' with respect to the suitability of each room for an overnight stay—character and capability may merge. So too when a firm commits to a statistical measure of performance—like Caterpillar's 48-hour worldwide spare-parts availability, Maytag's 10 years' trouble-free operation, Frito-Lay's 99.5 percent service level, or Domino's Pizza's 30-minute delivery. Simple, quantified standards of this sort raise two issues that any mission must address: how well ought the organization to do, and relative to whom or what?

REFERENCE GROUP
AND PERFORMANCE LEVEL

If character, customers, and capabilities define the corporate player's overall game, then the points of comparison that this organization uses make up its reference group, its "league." Every organization is in a league. In fact most are in several. To determine *which* leagues your company is in, ask yourself what other firms you reference organizational behavior/outcomes against.

In addition to knowing its game and its league, your organization needs to know how to keep score and what constitutes a "win." It needs to know how closely it is approximating its espoused mission. Quantitative measures of performance are essential.

I have played countless rounds of golf since I took up the sport when I was 11 years old. I have always played better when I kept score. Business is no different in this respect. Bob Swiggett, former CEO of Kollmorgen Company, summed it up this way: "People like to play hard and bet on the score of the games they play. The people who know what score it takes to win will always outperform those who don't."[4]

Perhaps few other companies have taken the business-as-a-game philosophy further than Springfield Remanufacturing Center Corp. (SRC), formerly a division of International Harvester Corp. and described by *Inc.* (in 1986) as "one of America's most competitive small companies." SRC is a thoroughgoing yet harmonious blend of players and scoreboards. According to SRC's president and largest shareholder, John P. Stack, "When you walk through this factory, you hear numbers everywhere you go. It's like you're in the middle of a bingo tournament." Stack explains his reason for rendering SRC as game-like as possible: "I just felt that, if you were going to spend a majority of your time doing a job, why couldn't you have fun at it? For me, fun was action, excitement, a good game. If there's one thing common to everybody, it's that we love to play a good game."[5]

Conceptually, your organization's league-and-score-board—its performance referents—can match any one or mix of the following four cells (Figure 5.1): An organization in cell 1 has as its standard its own history; its "league" is its predecessor organizations. Where such a past is storied, the standard may be ambitious indeed. Sports teams provide some obvious examples—for example, Earl Weaver's Baltimore Orioles, Vince Lombardi's Green Bay Packers, and Red Auerbach's Boston Celtics. Although business has its analogues—like Textron under Royal Little, UPS under James Casey and George Smith, and Doyle Dane Bernbach under William Bernbach—an organization's own past performance is often a weak yardstick. Thus when we see ads like those for General Motors' 1980 cars that boast "a 40% average fuel-economy improvement over 1975 models," we are seeing a very limited comparison. The same is true of the 1986 U.S. Postal Service ad for its Express Mail® service,

Figure 5.1. Types of Performance Referents

		PAST	FUTURE
	EXTERNAL	3	4
FOCUS			
	INTERNAL	1	2

TIME ORIENTATION

which assures users that "you're getting our best service ever . . . overnight reliability . . . of over 97%." In neither case do we know how such performance stacks up against the competition.

Looking backward may not only limit one's view of the degree of performance possible; more important, it may distort the very nature of performance required in the future. Yesterday it was the railroads whose rear-view tunnel vision did them in. Today, some believe it is primary metals. In a 1982 article about faltering Phelps Dodge Corp., *Business Week* cited "management's unswerving view that copper's future would always reflect copper's past and that its markets would continue to grow."[6] Historical referents are especially dangerous when they are rooted in the physical, as opposed to functional, properties of products—as companies wedded to vacuum tubes, carbon paper, and bias-ply tires have well demonstrated.

Next to business, team sports change precious little year to year. While comparisons with the past are admittedly problematic in sports, such comparisons are far more dicey in the corporate arena. Hence, cell 3 organizations—though their compass may be wider than that of organizations in cell 1—are vulnerable to flawed comparisons. Minimally, such comparisons tend to be restricted—like Ford's 1987 claim that "For seven years running . . . [it] has designed and built the highest-quality *American* cars and trucks" (emphasis added). Maximally, the comparisons are inappropriate. Firms bent on competing with the past are likely to become corporate equivalents of the negative military stereotype: forever preparing to fight the last war. To avoid just such a fate, Reginald Jones went out of his way to pick someone very different from himself—Jack Welch—as his successor at GE.

A corporation in cell 2 looks forward, but inward. Its emphasis is more on the potential than the historical. At the same time, the reference group is not made up of adversaries "out there," but of a spirit "in here." Edwin P. Land, the founder of Polaroid, expressed this perspective economically and eloquently: "Our competition is our own sense of excellence."[7] More recently, Ferrari advertisements state simply that "We are the competition."

Cell 4 organizations are forward- and outward-directed. Their field of vision may take in an increasing variety of referents. Unlike American auto companies that have—at least until very recently—restricted their comparisons to other American auto companies, cell 4 firms tend to open things up. They likely have something in common with Al Davis, the owner of the Los Angeles (née Oakland) Raiders, who has never been satisfied with superiority in pro football, or indeed, all of football. For some time Davis has wanted the comparative net cast wider: "I always wanted to build the finest organization in sports. . . . I'd have the greatest players, the greatest coaches. We'd play the greatest games. And someone would say, 'That's the best organization in sports.' I wanted it to be the ultimate."[8]

For most if not all organizations, the "appropriate" vantage is probably all of the cells—though the proportions will vary. In fact, a revealing exercise is to have each team member assess the relative influence of the four quadrants on current organizational thinking—by spreading 100 percentage points among the quadrants—and then to compare scores.

Each perspective has value. It may be as dangerous not to look back—not to see where you are coming from—as not to look forward. And it is a mistake to dismiss either internal standards or external rivals. John Wooden, who led UCLA basketball teams to an unprecedented 10 NCAA championships, seven of them consecutive, captured the importance of integrating internal and external in his description of "success" in basketball: "Success in coaching or playing should not be based on the number of games won or lost, but rather on the basis of what each individual does in relation to his own ability and in comparison with others when taking into consideration individual abilities, available facilities for use, the caliber of the opponents, the site of the contest, and other things of a similar nature."[9]

The list of external referents for the corporate player is nearly without limit. Some obvious possibilities:

- Relevant competitors (local or global, actual or potential)

- Organizations of equivalent or desired size

- Organizations of the same or desired ownership type

- Organizations with the same or desired growth trajectory

- Organizations with the same or desired functional emphasis

- Organizations with the same or desired technology/resource base

- Organizations at the same or desired "center of gravity" [that is, the approximate location in an industry's sequence of stages, ranging from far upstream (where raw materials/resources are acquired) to far downstream (the point at which the final product or service is used/consumed)[10]

- Organizations with a similar or desired "R&D multiplier" ("the ratio of R&D investment required to develop a product to the capital necessary to make and sell it.")[11]

- Organizations in the same community

- Peer units in the same corporation

- Model performers ("excellent" organizations by whatever criteria)

An interesting combination of model performer and functional emphasis is a practice known as "benchmarking"—comparing one's performance in a particular function or specialty with that of an outsider, often from a different industry. Xerox Corporation has used this practice since 1979. Its Logistics and Distribution unit, in particular, has made benchmarking a permanent routine. This unit wanted a fix on the best practices in warehouse operations. Where to turn? L. L. Bean, the outdoor clothier and mail-order firm. According to an article in the *Harvard Business Review,* "To the layperson, L. L. Bean products may bear no resemblance to Xerox parts and supplies. To the distribution professional, however, the analogy was striking: both companies had to develop warehousing and distribution systems to handle products diverse in size, shape, and weight. This diversity precluded the use of ASRS [automated storage and retrieval systems]."[12]

MISSION–DESIGN OVERLAP

A mission statement that *cannot* be translated into action is fraudulent; a statement that *is not* translated into action is sterile. But how can a statement be so translated if the organizational design to which it applies is not matched with it? The answer is that it cannot.

Conceptually and practically, mission and design are inseparable. They represent the dovetailing of organizational intention and intentional organization. Figure 5.2 depicts the primary areas of overlap between mission and design.

Mission and design imply each other. We cannot make statements about organizational character without at the same time addressing every component of design—organizational strategy, structure, and style. The same is true about

Figure 5.2. Mission/Design Overlap

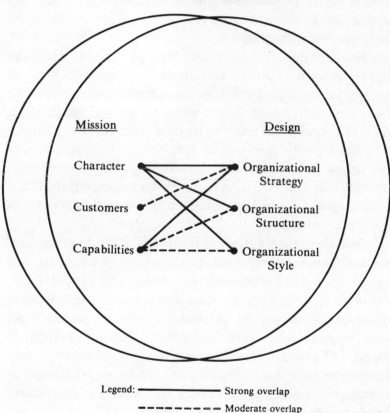

capabilities, where the intersection with organizational strategy is especially strong. Likewise, any statements about the nature of organizational design invariably touch on mission.

The area of least overlap appears to be the "customers" category of mission in relation to organizational design in general. But even this category links up with design. "Customers" refers not just to the organization's products and markets and clientele, but also to the routes chosen for new-business development—acquisition, internal processes, and/ or joint ventures. This category thus overlaps "developmental patterns" under organizational strategy, where the options are to develop from the outside, from within, and/ or in concert with others.[13]

The challenge for every corporate player is to craft the right composite mission and design. Once developed, of course, this amalgam must match the environment. But the fact of an environmental mismatch does not necessarily mean that the organization needs to be revamped. As Henry Mintzberg has argued, "The way to deal with the right structure in the wrong environment may be to change the environment, not the structure. Often, in fact, it is far easier to shift industries or retreat to a suitable niche in an industry than to undo a cohesive structure."[14]

Consider Japan's Brother Industries, Ltd. As consultant Kenichi Ohmae has reported, this company leveraged its core knowledge base to compete in an entirely new product/market domain. Originally a sewing machine company, Brother observed that sewing was becoming a dying art among Japanese women, who were increasingly buying ready-made clothes. The firm decided to apply its skills in microelectronics and precision machining to a new market—office automation. In short order, Brother became a leading manufacturer of electronic typewriters and printers.[15]

THE PROCESS
OF MISSION ARTICULATION

More organizations have a mission statement than have a systematic picture of their design. If a mission statement is available, then the first question is how accurately and completely it describes the organization's *actual* character, customers, and capabilities. How clear is the management team about its organizational reference group and its performance expectations? In the best-case scenario, the mission statement requires no additions, deletions, or changes. Short of this unlikely prospect, the mission statement needs either to be reworked to reflect reality, or to be worked up from scratch.

The key consideration in (re)drafting current mission is to lay things out the way they are, with utmost candor. The statement that is finally generated need not be smooth—in fact, probably *shouldn't* be smooth, because attending to style at this point would be a waste of time. Rather, your team should concentrate on creating as honest and revealing a depiction as possible without regard to wordsmithing.

If your team consists of eight or more people, it is probably wise to break into smaller groups and have each attempt to verbalize current mission. (A team of 12 or more may want to divide into three groups.) The sub-teams should then reconvene and each present its impression of current organizational mission. Wherever possible, the sub-teams' products should be synthesized into a common statement. If differences persist, then these need to be worked through. Once the team believes that its overall characterization is sufficiently consistent and complete, the task becomes one of assessing the fit between actual mission and actual organizational design.

Actual mission and organizational design will not necessarily always be closely aligned, any more than the major aspects of actual design—strategy, structure, and style—will be parallel. At this point, however, what matters is objectivity, not symmetry. Such is not the case with *re*design, where consistency—within organizational design, and between design and mission—is critical.

Chapter Six

Redesigning
Your Organization

Having articulated current mission and completed the Teamwork Profile at least twice—first individually, then collectively (and perhaps a third time, in concert with others)—the management team probably has its clearest picture ever of what the organization is and what it stands for. The next step is to design the desired organization.

What *should* your organization's mission be? What *should* its design be? There may be an organization somewhere out there in which actual mission/design does correspond exactly to the desired. But I have never observed such an instance, nor do I know anyone else who has. The closest thing to a match that I have encountered involved about 20 insurance agents and a major financial services company with which they were affiliated. These agents, who in effect were independent contractors, were the highest producers for the larger firm. They were the "crème de la crème," as one senior manager put it. After conducting a half-day workshop with the group, I learned why their actual teamwork blend was remarkably close to what they desired: Each individual was so successful and so mobile that if a mismatch had existed, he or she likely would have simply ended the affiliation rather than investing energy in trying to change things (or putting up with an undesirable arrangement). As one participant explained, "We're not like the typical employee in a corporation who is more or less stuck with their game." This collection of individuals clearly was an exceptional case.

In general, the charge to team members is to come up with a constraint-free vision, or what Russell Ackoff calls an idealized system redesign—namely, one "with which the designers would *now* replace the existing system if they were free to replace it with any system they wanted."[1] As with the diagnosis of the current organization, it makes little difference whether mission or organizational design is the lead item. In either case the team will almost certainly have to cycle back and forth between the two.

The initial design process should be similar to that used for the diagnosis, as explained in Chapter 4. Each individual completes the Teamwork Profile and translates his or her numbers onto the Teamwork Triangle. Everyone's summary assessments are combined on a single Triangle. As a team, you then work through each dimension of the Profile, agreeing wherever possible and making a record of any continuing disagreements. It is likely that by the time your team has completed a first pass through both organizational design and mission, some differences will remain. If these are substantive, you may want to draft two or three alternative mission/design statements and debate the merits of each over a period of weeks or even months. Chances are that team members eventually will be able to agree on a concept that integrates features of the various alternatives.

Once your team has achieved consensus on a desired mission/organizational design, it needs to consider the change options available for approaching this state. As we will see shortly, the management team may have considerable choice in routes.

TWO-PHASE DESIGN PROCESS

The process just outlined constitutes the first of two interacting design phases: *conceptualization*, in which your team (1) paints a portrait of what it would like the organization to be, irrespective of how difficult it may be to realize this state, and (2) considers alternative change trajectories. Your conceptualization is driven by a shared vision of a desired future, by perceptions of opportunity, and by some measure of necessity. The second design phase is concerned with *commitment*: in broad terms, what future you will select and what it will take to get there. Commitment is heavily influenced by your team's sense of its own and the larger organization's capacity for change: To what extent are people ready and able to move? How fast and how far? The commitment phase provides your team with a second chance, with the opportunity to revise the desired organizational future that was articulated during phase one. It is thus a reality check as well as a spelling out of more detail. Conceptualization is the primary concern of this chapter; commitment is the subject of Chapter 7.

The logic underpinning the two-phase design process is analogous to that behind brainstorming. Brainstorming involves two very different behaviors, in train. First, participants *div*erge. They go out of their way to generate as many alternatives as possible. No evaluation or criticism is permitted until the group has exhausted itself of ideas. At that point, participants *con*verge. They systematically assess the options and eventually come up with as logical and acceptable a course of action as possible. Divergence is based on letting imagination have free rein; convergence is grounded in hard, rational thinking. It is the combination of these modes, in sequence, that makes brainstorming so effective.

So too with the design process. The key during conceptualization is not to impose limits on yourselves when you envision a desired future—in other words, to be freed up so that you come up with the best conceivable design and consider all the options for getting there. Team members need to diverge from normal thinking patterns, which are so often influenced by concerns about what is practical or politic. But this phase is not sufficient. It must be followed up with an expression of personal commitment by team members, individually and collectively. Such commitment represents a convergence on the level of effort and degree of resources that will be expended in order to move the organization in the direction of its desired future. As in brainstorming, it is the *combination* that makes all the difference. But where the design process differs from brainstorming is in its interactive character. Initially, conceptualization precedes commitment, but the flow then becomes two-way. Your team may well revise its conceptualization after testing it against the resource levels that it implies. In a nutshell, conceptualization and commitment modify each other. Their product is the most ambitious design to which the organization can be committed.

For now, let's concentrate on conceptualization. After having reached at least a tentative agreement on desired future, the next step for the team is to contrast this vision with the organization's current state. The difference can be summarized visually on the Teamwork Triangle by using the conversion guidelines presented in Chapter 4, and reproduced below in Figure 6.1.

The Teamwork Triangle will reveal possible problems about the *degree* of teamwork present or sought, as well as the *nature* of teamwork. Each shaded area represents a vulnerable pattern. The shaded corners indicate that a particular kind of teamwork—whether appropriate or not—may be overdone; the shaded center triangle suggests that teamwork priorities are understated—are not sufficiently clear.

VULNERABLE STRATEGIES

Too Much Autonomy

Consider some situations that appear to fall within the shaded areas. Autonomy becomes problematic when a relatively freestanding part—individual or organizational unit—

Figure 6.1. Converting Scores to the Teamwork Triangle

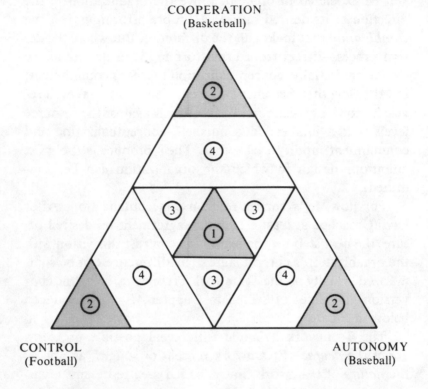

COOPERATION
(Basketball)

CONTROL
(Football)

AUTONOMY
(Baseball)

Legend:
① All three column totals virtually equal

② One column dominant

③ Two columns dominant

④ None of the above (significant differences between highest, middle, and lowest totals)

overdoes its own thing. The motion picture industry provides a surfeit of examples. According to author Steven Bach, who was fired from United Artists after *Heaven's Gate* flopped, "The deep paradox in Hollywood is that artists are given *too much* freedom, not because of a deep respect executives have for artists but because of indifference. It's a laissez-faire kind of thing."[2]

But Hollywood has no monopoly on centrifugal tendencies. People who are given wide latitude tend to go their own way—whether they are investment bankers at Drexel Burnham, elite editors at Simon & Schuster, or star scientists at Xerox's Palo Alto Research Center (PARC). Charles Simonyi, a former researcher at PARC, explained an exodus of prominent scientists from that organization in this way: "Xerox brought together very high-powered people, very much the stars in their fields. But how do you expect them to work together? Stars of a certain brightness tend to explode."[3] Minimally, excessive autonomy within a corporation can lead to fragmentation, to lack of organizational coherence; more seriously, it can result in individuals' putting their customers, clients, geographical sites, or technical disciplines ahead of corporate interests.

Conglomerates are frequently faulted for overdiversifying, for becoming a motley collection of businesses that have no common strands. And, as I indicated earlier (Chapter 5), there is evidence that the more disparate a corporation's range of operations, the more poorly it is likely to perform. The same tendency toward diffuseness can be found in nonconglomerates as well. Kollmorgen Corporation became a media darling only a few years ago when it decentralized into 14 autonomous divisions. But in short order it became apparent that, in the face of a severe downturn in the electronics industry, divisional autonomy had been overdone. Said CEO Jim Swiggett in late 1986: "I suppose what went wrong is that things were going so well that we didn't pay enough attention to the changing fundamentals of the economy and of our industry. And as a result, we found ourselves going off in too many different directions. . . . And our enthusiasm for running a largely decentralized organization, with its high level of entrepreneurial orientation—that caused us to get ourselves spread too thin. We had become overenthusiastic about the idea of corporate regeneration."[4]

Too Much Control

Now let's consider control. We need not look very far to find examples of organizational failure that are at least partly attributable to overcontrol. Virtually any rust-belt/smokestack mainstay—steel, autos, rubber, and the office equivalent, whitecollar bureaucracy—is rife with tales of woe that stem from concentrated control. In fact, control serves as the fundamental counterpoint for virtually all forays into participative management. Harvard's Richard Walton has put the matter as a binary opposition: control versus commitment.[5]

Top-down control is most workable in stable environments, and this is the root of its vulnerability. The more controlled an organization becomes, the more finely attuned it will be to the needs of its current environmental niche. Such environmental "fit" is what ecologists refer to as *adaptation*. The problem is that adaptation comes at the expense of *adaptability*—the capacity to adapt to new environments.[6]

Ford Motor Co. learned the hard way about the costs of nonadaptability—and overcontrol—when, several years ago, it had to permanently close its most automated plant. The plant had become so "dedicated" to operations linked to eight-cylinder engines that when market conditions began to favor six cylinders, it was unable to change.[7] Similarly, Deere & Co. in 1986 had to shut down—temporarily, at least—its only U.S. tractor and harvester facility (in Waterloo, Iowa) as a combined result of a labor dispute and a soft market. The underlying difficulty? According to *Business Week*,

"The heavily robotized production process is so closely integrated that it is virtually impossible to shut down one part of the operation without shutting everything down."[8]

Inherent in nonadaptability is a limited concept of human resources. Since highly controlled organizations rely on the wisdom and guidance of the top manager—or planner or system designer—the skills and initiative of others throughout the organization tend to be underdeveloped and underused. Generalist skills receive scant attention. At the extreme, it is as if people are viewed as little cogs, with carefully bounded functions that are meshed from above to produce organizational clockwork.

Too Much Cooperation

Like autonomy and control, cooperation can be overdone. As helpful as it may be to break down organizational barriers, relying on informal relations can be taken too far. A prime example is Convergent Technologies' failed attempt to produce a lap-model portable computer, dubbed "Workslate." Early on, Karen Tolland, Workslate's marketing manager, praised the flexibility of the development process: "I don't have to go through two department heads and write six memos if something needs to be changed. I just walk across the hall and say, 'Hey, Charlie, this space bar feels like . . . and then he fixes it.'"[9] Less than a year later, however, the danger of this informality had become painfully clear. Workslate was scrapped before it ever got off the ground. In retrospect, Tolland admitted the need for a more rigorous process: "We were under tremendous pressure to ship the product and simply didn't have enough time . . . [to go] through the usual intermediate stage in which products are fully tested, refined, and streamlined."[10]

Another difficulty with cooperative processes is the decision overload they can generate. It is simply not possible to have intensive back-and-forth exchanges among all individuals in large groups or organizations. In most cases, the maximum number of people that can engage in a consensual decision-making process is probably about 12 to 15; in my own experience, once double figures are reached the process is apt to become laborious. Likewise for organizations. It is fine to rely on informal, face-to-face relations when the organization is small and everyone knows everyone else. But as growth takes place, the limits to voluntary cooperation quickly become apparent. Although I can't hazard an organizational number that corresponds to a group number, I can certainly identify corporate examples that have exceeded the limits. One that immediately springs to mind is People Express Airlines. As another CEO remarked about People CEO Donald Burr in early 1985—long before that ill-fated carrier's troubles were front-page news—"He's passed a point of critical mass. There's a point where structure counts."[11]

In late 1986 Lufthansa, West Germany's state-run airline, was another example of cooperative processes taken too far. Consensus had degenerated into bureaucracy. Claimed one senior manager, "We have too many cumbersome decisions by consensus. It's difficult to get someone to take responsibility for a decision." Lufthansa then announced plans to restructure into route-based profit centers, each headed by a single manager—a move intended, among other things, to fix accountability. Said another company spokesperson at the time: "Today, there is no one in the company but the top six men collectively responsible for, say, North Atlantic routes."[12]

I have yet to observe the management team at any level that can function in an entirely consensual mode. The paradox that many team-builders seem to miss is that in order for there to be cooperation, there must also be some measure of autonomy and some measure of control. In decision-making terms, one cannot effectively collaborate if he or she does not also delegate and mandate. But it is dangerous to attempt to do all three in equal measure.

Stuck in the Middle

An organization stuck in the middle triangle is unclear about its teamwork priorities.[13] Such a conundrum is more subtle than overdoing any particular form of teamwork, in part because every organization does need to blend the three pulls. One of the most graphic descriptions of being stuck that I have heard was applied to a billion-dollar company unable to align its fundamental strategy, structure, and style. As one frustrated manager expressed it, "We're a football structure trying to compete in a basketball business by relying on baseball players."

The top management team of another firm with which I am familiar unknowingly expressed its absence of team priorities in a draft vision statement that was intent on making the corporation all things. In just one sentence, this group "committed" itself to developing a culture characterized by creativity, innovation, efficiency, direction, flexibility, and risk-taking. A culture, in other words, that would simultaneously maximize individual autonomy, top-down control, and spontaneous cooperation. That's all, folks.

On a less grand scale we find the company or division or business unit trying for the best of all three worlds not simultaneously, but in succession. Last month (or quarter, or year) the rallying cry was "Individual initiative and accountability"; this period it is "Consistency, consistency, consistency"; next period it will be "Cooperate to compete." Such an organization lurches from one competitive criterion to another without ever establishing a coherent pattern. Small wonder that people feel permanently at sea.

THREE CHANGE ROUTES

Your organization has these change options for moving from its current state to a more desirable future: adjustment, transition, or transformation. (A fourth option, of course, is to do nothing.) Adjustment is the least ambitious of the three alternatives: The organization's design is fine-tuned, either to keep it the same or to nudge it back to a former and still-workable state. Transition represents gradual, orderly change to a new design. Transformation denotes radical change to a new design. In a word, adjustment is concerned with *equilibrium*, transition with *evolution*, and transformation with *revolution*. These three options are arrayed along a continuum in Figure 6.2.

Figure 6.2. A Change Continuum

ADJUSTMENT (Equilibrium-seeking)	TRANSITION (Evolutionary)	TRANSFORMATION (Revolutionary)
Continuous		Discontinuous
Piecemeal		Systematic
Local		Global
Reversible		Irreversible
Efficiency-based		Effectiveness-based
Quantitative		Qualitative
Tactical		Strategic
Requiring marginal resources		Requiring substantial resources

Which option makes the most sense for your organization? A general guide is provided by the following matrix (Figure 6.3), which lines up Teamwork Triangle data—the gap between actual and desired designs—with the three change options. As a rule, adjustment never requires crossing a line in the Teamwork Triangle; transition may or may not involve crossing one line; and transformation always requires crossing two or more lines. By implication, an organization cannot extricate itself from a vulnerable position (shaded area) simply by "adjusting." More serious change is necessary.

If your actual organization falls within the shaded center triangle—"stuck in the middle"—then you may be faced with the need for either a transition or a transformation, depending on what kind of organization you desire. Similarly, if your actual organization represents the wrong design but does not fall within one of the shaded areas, then either a transition or a transformation may be necessary—again depending on where you want the organization to be.

Figure 6.3, like any other organizational-change matching scheme, is meant to be suggestive, not authoritative. Attempting to use it in a mechanical way would be naive and dangerous. Rather, the matrix is intended to help you think about generic change alternatives in the context of your own organization's situation and aspirations.

Adjustment

No change alternative—including doing nothing—is without risk. The chief danger with adjustment is that it amounts to trivial change—tweaking the organization when something more than a pinch is required. Many companies' experiences with quality circles fit this category. More generally, quality-

Figure 6.3. Change Matrix

CHANGE OPTION / ACTUAL DESIGN (in Relation to Desired Design	Adjustment	Transition	Transformation*
Right teamwork priority, White area of Teamwork Triangle	X	X	
Right teamwork priority, Shaded area of Teamwork Triangle		X	
No clear teamwork priority (Shaded center of Teamwork Triangle)		X	X
Wrong teamwork priority, White area of Teamwork Triangle		X	X
Wrong teamwork priority, Shaded area of Teamwork Triangle			X

*Or Multiple Transitions, as discussed below.

of-work-life initiatives—to the extent that they never seriously engage middle-to-senior managers—constitute little more than organizational adjustment, no matter how novel or apparently successful they may be. The same is true of conventional team-building—even among middle-to-senior managers—if, as is usually the case, this activity fails to get beyond matters of style. Having led team-building sessions with a wide array of organizational units, I believe that expectations should be modest unless such activity is combined with strategic/structural change. Figure 6.4 shows typical ef-

Figure 6.4. Typical Effects of Team-Building as a Stand-Alone Program

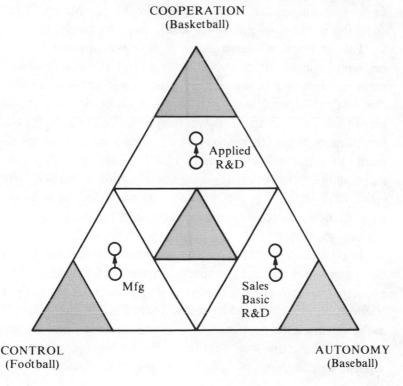

COOPERATION
(Basketball)

Applied
R&D

Mfg

Sales
Basic
R&D

CONTROL
(Football)

AUTONOMY
(Baseball)

fects of team-building as a stand-alone program—that is, with no connection to more substantive change.

"Charitable Foundation" is a generic name for an organization to which a colleague, Frank Farrow, and I consulted over several months during 1985–86. The presenting problem was management's concern about the future performance of the foundation's grant processing and tracking system in light of an expanding work load, increasingly long grant periods, and changing personnel. Upon analysis, it was clear that what "system" problems existed were more basically organizational problems. Specifically, we discovered that the administrative system charged with monitoring the grant process had become needlessly bureaucratic. Program units had to contend with a pile of forms and with a set of procedures that emphasized checking, rechecking, and more rechecking at multiple points by administrative personnel.

This state of affairs mirrored an organizational schism between program units (which carried out the foundation's main mission of making quality grants) and the administrative unit (which both supported the program units and scrutinized their performance). A we/they attitude had developed. Program units saw themselves as similar to academic departments in a university: concerned with planning, reflection, learning, peer networking—in general, with concepts. The administrative unit perceived itself more or less as a bank. Its province was control, scheduling, and the financials—in essence, numbers.

Everyone recognized that the foundation needed to blend autonomy and control (cooperation was not at issue). The problem was how to do this in a way that reflected proper foundation priorities and at the same time minimized internal antagonisms. Our proposal, which was accepted and implemented, had two key features. First, we recommended separating program and administrative control spheres temporally by making program personnel responsible for grant-*making* activities and administrative personnel responsible for grant-*control* activities. The dividing line was the point at which a grant was approved for funding. Second, we suggested that program units be provided additional support staff so that they would have self-control capability through all of the steps leading up to grant approval—previously the bailiwick of the administrative unit.

By taking these measures, Charitable Foundation effectively restored its teamwork priority balance—the distance between autonomy, its first priority, and control—to the arrangement that had existed before the administrative mechanism became bureaucratized. Change involved not a reordering of priorities but a reweighting. Indeed, even while excessive administrative controls were in effect, the program units still had primacy over the administrative unit—a fact brought home by the independence and very different styles that program managers displayed throughout. Charitable Foundation thus "adjusted" by undertaking modest change that nonetheless was appropriate and adequate. Figure 6.5 captures this adjustment.

Transition

Trammell Crow Co., the nation's largest real estate firm (total assets in excess of $13 billion as of February 1987) illustrates a different direction and a different process from Charitable Foundation.[14] Trammell Crow had for years been famous for the autonomy of its regional partners. Then, in early 1987, the company announced moves designed to tighten headquarters' control. The actions taken constituted a clear transition.

Crow consolidated commercial and real estate opera-

Figure 6.5. Adjustment at Charitable Foundation

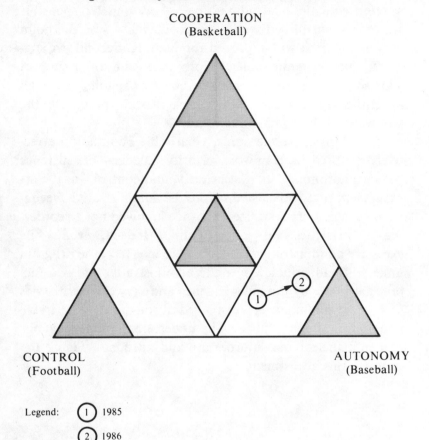

COOPERATION
(Basketball)

CONTROL
(Football)

AUTONOMY
(Baseball)

Legend: ① 1985
② 1986

tions, and other activities. Senior partners in the Dallas home office were vested with voting control of the organization, and their take from real estate transactions was increased. An extra hierarchical level, made up of younger partners, was created. College recruiting became coordinated by a single individual.

Why such moves? Autonomy had begun to get out of

hand—especially at a time when real estate companies were feeling a cost squeeze and facing the prospect of office vacancy rates as high as 25 percent nationwide.[15] In certain cities, different divisions competed with each other—as was also the case on elite university campuses, where recruits were being wooed by competing Crow units. Much of the difficulty stemmed from Crow's size. The company's spectacular growth—a quintupling over the last 10 years—had required, in the words of managing partner Joel Peterson, "an evolution, a break from the way we've done things." Peterson continued: "We thought it was important to get control of the Trammell Crow name. It's been necessary to recognize the size that we are." Trammell Crow was responding as much to tomorrow as to today. Although its performance to date had been impressive, the firm was concerned about its ability to accommodate future growth. Figure 6.6 depicts Trammell Crow's Transition.

An organization opting for transition may suffer from either of two opposite tendencies: moving faster/further than conditions warrant (when at most, adjustment is indicated) or moving too tentatively/conservatively (when transformation is necessary). Many cases of moving too slowly reflect an inability to come to grips with new technology—for example, American Viscose's failure to replace rayon tire cord with nylon, or Transitron's failure to replace germanium transistors with silicon.[16] Such technological changes usually require radically altering the organization.

People Express' famous demise may reflect either action that was too bold or action that was not bold enough—or perhaps both. Its late-1985 acquisition of Frontier Airlines struck many observers as precipitous and incongruous—a transition of exactly the wrong kind, for two reasons. First, from a size standpoint, People Express was already straining the capabilities of its informal, free-form style; adding a ma-

Figure 6.6. Transition at Trammell Crow

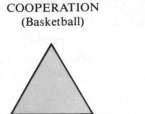

COOPERATION
(Basketball)

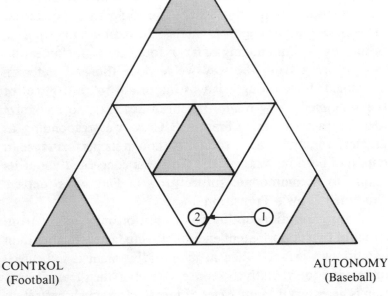

CONTROL
(Football)

AUTONOMY
(Baseball)

Legend: ① Pre-1987

② 1987

jor airline was like throwing gasoline on a fire. Second, (unionized) Frontier Airlines was the antithesis of (nonunion) People Express—conventional, hierarchical, and inflexible.

At the same time, quite apart from the Frontier deal, People seemed in dire need of transitional change that would respond to the demands of its increased size and complexity. In 1984, social scientist Richard Hackman published an analysis of People Express's first two and one-half years, titled "The Transition That Hasn't Happened."[17] Hackman offered several alternative explanations for the absence of a transition at People. He then wondered: "So what do we have here? An organization that has merely put off its inevitable transition for a time—and will pay the price for it later? Or one that managed to get through its period of vulnerability to transitional processes relatively unscathed by them? Or one that is transcending the conventional dynamics of organizational growth and development? Or is there yet another way of understanding the absence of significant transitions at People Express, one that has eluded this observer?"

But at the end point of Hackman's study, People Express was barely over half the age it would be when it bought Frontier. And it had fewer than 1,800 employees, as against more than 4,000 in late 1985 at the time of the acquisition. Looking at things from a distance, without being privy to the internal goings-on, it seems that considerably more of an organizational transition was called for than People ever mounted, irrespective of the extent to which Donald Burr and People may have redefined conventional organizational dynamics. In the absence of such transition—and disregarding the purchase of Frontier—People Express appeared to have drifted into excessive reliance on informal, voluntary cooperation, as illustrated by Figure 6.7.

A contrasting example to People Express is Tandem Computers, which in 1985–86 managed to correct its earlier tendency to overplay the right game.[18] In the late 1970s Tandem was a highflier; its sales and profits doubled annually from 1976 until 1981. Under CEO James Treybig, it became widely celebrated as a model of participative management. Then came four years of lackluster performance: depressed margins, flat earnings, and lowered stock prices.

To turn things around, Treybig made significant product-

Figure 6.7. Drift at People Express (Sans Frontier Airlines)

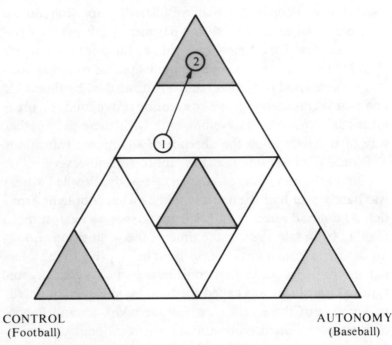

COOPERATION
(Basketball)

CONTROL
(Football)

AUTONOMY
(Baseball)

Legend: ① 1982-83
         ② 1985-86

line and marketing changes. He also did some organizational tightening by strengthening control systems and squeezing out production efficiencies. On top of this, Treybig took much more of a hands-on approach to operations than he had in the past—even going so far as to relocate his office in different departments in order to oversee what was going on.

Treybig also took a stand on reward systems in the face of sagging morale when he froze salary levels and halted sales incentive plans. Observed vice president Gerald D. Held, "Jim made the transition from team member to president."[19] Put another way, he went from PLAYER/coach to player/COACH.

Yet when performance returned to past high levels, Tandem's style followed suit. Reported *Business Week* in early 1987: "With the good times back, so is the old Tandem spirit, thanks in large part to a worldwide electronic mail system and in-house TV network that Treybig uses to keep in touch with employees. All the previous trappings of company culture, such as swimming pools, paid sabbaticals, and Friday afternoon beer busts, are still around, too—and more ingrained than ever."[20]

But Treybig has come to realize that informal communication is not sufficient for a company of over 6,000 employees spread across 130 locations. As he acknowledged about Tandem's communications in 1987, "It's all very structured. I spend a lot of time working on systems that allow the communication."[21] Tandem's journey from pre-1981 to 1987 is suggested by Figure 6.8.

James River Graphics, Inc., a subsidiary of Richmond-based James River Corporation, is a group of businesses whose mission is to "provide specialty coated products of **superior value** to customers primarily in the information materials and decorative products markets." Over the past nine years Graphics has evolved, through a series of transitions, in a way that may serve as a model for many other companies. Graphics has gone from a control-based organization, to an autonomy/control hybrid, to a near-equal blend of autonomy, control, and cooperation. Or, in more conventional organizational-design language, the firm has evolved from a

Figure 6.8. Drift and Transition at Tandem Computers

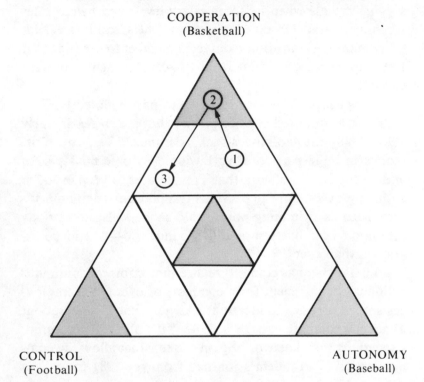

COOPERATION
(Basketball)

CONTROL
(Football)

AUTONOMY
(Baseball)

Legend: ① Prior to 1981
② 1982-85
③ 1986-87

functional structure, to a divisional structure, to a matrix. It now appears to be on its way out of the matrix and moving toward what I call an autonomy/cooperation hybrid.

James River acquired the Graphics operation from Scott Paper in 1978. At that time, Graphics was a classic functional bureaucracy, somewhat top-heavy and layered. James River streamlined the organization by eliminating a considerable number of middle-management positions. As the complexity facing the firm increased over the next three years, however, it became clear to group vice-president Karl V. Kraske and his Graphics' senior management team that a functional design, no matter how efficiently staffed, was not up to the task. Top functional managers were being spread too thin across an ever-expanding array of products, markets, and technologies. Accordingly, in 1981, Graphics split into two divisions, reflecting its two major product categories. Had Graphics divisionalized completely—that is, made each division a self-contained entity—then it could have been characterized as an autonomy-based company. But it never went that far. Too much resource duplication would have been required.

When I first became involved with Graphics, as an organizational consultant in spring 1983, the firm was still divisionalized but was feeling a number of organizational blockages. Divisional priorities often conflicted. Resolving disputes about such things as machine availability and maintenance priorities required a cumbersome process of hierarchical referral. Graphics' senior management believed that a more participative management style was called for. In design terms, this meant greater cooperation relative to both control (the prevailing mode for vertical relationships) and autonomy (the prevailing mode for horizontal relationships—that is, between divisions). In fact, an early exercise that the top 14 managers completed was to describe Graphics using a variation of the Teamwork Profile. The results? Managers overwhelmingly saw the place as a blend of baseball and football, with virtually no basketball being played. There was widespread feeling of negative organizational synergy—that somehow individuals were far more talented than their collective performance demonstrated. Everybody recognized the need for increased collaboration. As evidence of its commitment to playing the new game, the top team agreed to meet off-site for a total of 12 days over the next four months in order to articulate a mission and a set of behavioral principles emphasizing cooperation—and then to develop a plan to communicate this new direction to everyone else in the company.

A formal "Mission Statement and Principles" document was published, distributed, and discussed throughout the organization. "Employee involvement" orientations and team-building sessions were begun. All the while, the top management team continued to meet regularly, both to monitor progress and to reassess its own role in the cooperative process. In late 1984–early 1985, the top team embarked on structural changes that, combined with the stylistic changes already underway, amounted to an organizational transition.

The top team took three related steps. First, it reconstituted itself as the Management Operating Committee (MOC) and recognized its *collective* responsibility for strategically managing the entire enterprise. Second, the top team reorganized Graphics into a product/function matrix, with three strategic business units (each containing multiple product teams) along one dimension, and manufacturing, engineering, human resources, and administration along the other dimension. Third, and in support of the first two steps, Graphics' senior team developed a decision matrix that laid out decision-making authorities within the MOC and between this group and the rest of the organization. The decision matrix was a kind of road map for operating the matrix structure; it showed which decisions should be delegated, which mandated, and which collaborated in. This document then became integrated into the basic team-building menu and thus was spread down and across the organization.

As a combined result of internal growth and related acquisitions—involving some distant sites—Graphics now appears in transition beyond the matrix and towards a combination autonomy/cooperation hybrid. An early indication of this transition was a mid-1986 event that recognized both the accomplishments of the MOC and the fact that this body no longer represented the whole of Graphics, especially in light of the recent acquisitions. MOC members capped off their last "official" meeting with a round of golf and a dinner, at which it was announced that each member would receive a plaque commemorating the MOC as "Creators of Change, 1983–1986."

At this writing, the "Graphics Group" is made up of seven divisions, each headed by a vice president/general manager. Certain functions are group-wide; others are based in the divisions. Given the likelihood of Graphics' continued growth, increasing diversity, and greater geographical complexity, it seems probable that centralized control will diminish even further as a coordinating mechanism. Instead it can be expected that divisional autonomy will increase—but that at the same time, there will be greater reliance on the divisions to share resources *voluntarily*, that is, without direction from the top. In this connection it is noteworthy that team-building and other group process activities have continued to spread throughout Graphics as a complement to structural change. Figure 6.9 traces Graphics' evolution.

Two summary observations are in order. First, as Figure 6.9 illustrates, Graphics' movement from ① to ④ involves crossing three lines. It is highly doubtful that Graphics—or any other comparable organization—could have spanned this distance in one leap, through a quantum transformation. But this is not to say that the nine-year period could not have been compressed somewhat. Looking back, Karl Kraske said that "three to four years of the time line was consumed as we became fully aware of what was happening and while we developed new approaches."

Figure 6.9. Multiple Transitions at James River Graphics

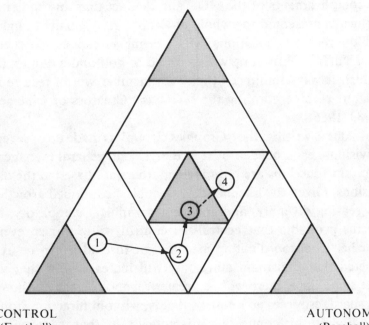

Legend:
- ① 1978 Acquisition
- ② 1981 Divisionalization
- ③ 1984-85 Matrix
- ④ 1987-Beyond: Possible Autonomy/Cooperation Hybrid

The second observation concerns matrix. I have suggested that this design option is "vulnerable." Yet Graphics acted wisely in adopting such a structure and has made it work. (Graphics' financial performance improved markedly after the organization had shifted into a matrix in 1985, and performance has remained strong since then.) Although I believe that a matrix design has long-term liabilities because of its tendency to muddle priorities, I also think that matrix can be an effective bridge between more stable designs—in this case, an autonomy/control hybrid (divisional structure) and an autonomy/cooperation hybrid. Since much of U.S. industry is confronting exactly this challenge—how to move from the familiar divisional model to an unfamiliar blend that treats cooperation as a partial substitute for control—perhaps James River Graphics' experience can provide some valuable insights.

Transformation

Organizational transformation has been a business buzzword for several years now. Writers and consultants alike have jumped onto the transformation bandwagon, arguing that conventional approaches to organization development and change are not enough in today's turbulent world. Indeed, there are instances in which transformation, as I am using the word,[22] is the only hope. But there are probably many more situations that are better confronted through multiple transitions—which may amount to phased transformation, or in the language of golf, doglegged change.

The primary danger that attends one-step transformation is exceeding the organization's capacity to change—as happened, for example, when Addressograph-Multigraph tried to soar nonstop from electromechanical to electronic technologies in the late 1970s, only to fail. In fact, an organization may be faced with a catch-22 in which any dramatic thrust is too much for people to handle, yet failure to take such a bold initiative is equally fatal.

A case of transformation that may or may not turn out to be a model for others to emulate is Gould Inc.'s rapid conversion from a manufacturer of such mundane products as batteries, electrical equipment, and bearings to a high-technology firm. Under former CEO William T. Ylvisaker, Gould in only five years rid itself of 22 old-line businesses and acquired 13 electronics companies. The issues, now as then, are pace and price. Admitted Gould executive vice-president Harry A. Caunter in mid-1986: "After $450 million in write-offs, I can guarantee we could have done it better."[23] But it may still be too early for anyone to render a definitive judgment about the speed of Gould's metamorphosis.

One lesson, however, can now be drawn from Gould's experience: It is possible to overshoot a desired future state—that is, to play too much of a new game. Ylvisaker reasoned, correctly, that high-tech calls for an essentially different style from smokestack. Gould's old-line businesses, he believed, required a heavy hand "because the innovative opportunities . . . are relatively small to build profit margins. The difference between success and failure is really very tight controls." With high-technology, by contrast, "it's a case of creating an atmosphere for those people where they have the freedom and the opportunity and the excitement of innovating, of getting those new products out, because product obsolescence in the business is anywhere from six months to two years today. So you've already got to be doing something new, and you can't legislate that. You've got to provide much higher incentives, greater freedom."[24]

Given this point of view, it is not surprising that Ylvisaker took several actions to reinforce his new entrepreneurs' autonomy. As *Business Week* reported in mid-1984, he relaxed top-down controls, compressed a corporate policy manual, trimmed corporate staff, granted planning authority to each unit, and gave general managers the freedom to commit to capital expenditures of up to $500,000 (versus a former ceiling of $10,000).[25] Two years later, Ylvisaker's successor as

CEO, James F. McDonald, had a very different task. Said *Business Week:* "Perhaps McDonald's biggest problem is reining in the company's new businesses. He inherited 22 undermanaged divisions that fanned out below him in relative independence."[26] In a sense, McDonald had to orchestrate a counter-transition made necessary by the Ylvisaker-induced transformation.

There is irony in Gould's scenario, what with a hardnosed industrial manager accustomed to mandating who overdoes the other extreme of delegating when faced with a new imperative. But there is another lesson as well: Mandating and delegating are only two-thirds of the mix; the remaining ingredient is collaborating. McDonald, who played basketball at the University of Kentucky, seems intuitively to have understood this. His early actions in correcting Ylvisaker's excesses had as much to do with engendering cooperation as with reasserting controls. Said Harry Caunter shortly after McDonald became CEO: "You walk away with a strong feeling that you participated in the decisions that were reached. Even if you didn't agree with them, you understand why they were made."[27] Figure 6.10 summarizes the trajectories that Gould appears to have taken since 1981.

The illustrations above are meant to provide perspective on the kinds of change possible. Your team may find it helpful to "pattern" other organizational change experiences with which it is familiar, using the Teamwork Profile and/or Triangle, in order to get a more concrete sense of what the different options entail. In any case, at this point you should have a good conceptual grasp of:

- The desired organization
- The gap between the desired organization and the actual organization
- Change alternatives for bridging this gap

Figure 6.10. Transformation and Counter-Transition at Gould

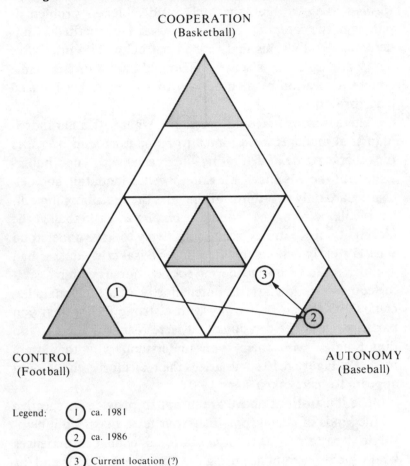

COOPERATION
(Basketball)

CONTROL
(Football)

AUTONOMY
(Baseball)

Legend: ① ca. 1981
② ca. 1986
③ Current location (?)

The task now before your team is commitment: What re-design *will* you pursue, and how? Commitment may thus imply reconceptualization of the desired organization, as your team may feel the need to scale back its aspirations. But whether or not the desired portrait is revised, commitment does imply specifying an action agenda—the subject of Chapter 7.

Chapter Seven

Making It Happen

Chapter 6 was concerned with conceptualizing the change process. The present chapter concentrates on the commitment necessary to make it happen. Everyone has heard the platitude that management commitment is central to successful organizational change. But commitment means different things to different people at different times, and the only commitment to be trusted is that whose cost can be gauged. As corporate culture and "visioning" have become fashionable over the last few years, a wave of firms have spawned statements of mission, philosophy, shared values, and guiding principles. Each has constructed a verbal edifice. But what has it all meant? In the majority of cases, probably not much.

The disparity between intention and behavior is understandable. We all know that actions speak louder than words. But the root difficulty lies deeper. Our American culture historically has assumed that language should *mirror* reality—that is, should come after it. We have an inherent distrust of the notion that it is legitimate to articulate words in advance of the behavior they are supposed to represent. This distrust is in sharp contrast to the Confucian notion of the *reification of names,* which, according to Paul Watzlawick et al., "is based on the belief that from the 'right' name the 'right' reality should follow—rather than assuming, as we do in the West, that names *reflect* reality."[1] Watzlawick and his coauthors show how the Red Guards applied the reification concept during the early stages of the Chinese Cultural Revolution by replacing the "bourgeois" names of all public signs—of streets, buildings, and so on—with revolutionary names.

When a corporation publishes a vision or mission statement that differs from and "leads" desired behavior, it is attempting to do what the Red Guards did in Mao's China: put *intention ahead of action,* but without cultural acceptance of the process. No wonder so many of these documents are ineffectual. Much of the vision/mission phenomenon amounts to a reversal of the experiences of "model" corporations, in which entrepreneurs/founders/early leaders—like Thomas Watson and Thomas Watson, Jr., of IBM, Robert W. Johnson of Johnson & Johnson, William Hewlett of Hewlett-Packard, and Kenneth Olsen of Digital Equipment—put *action ahead of intention* by reinforcing patterns of behavior long before these were ever codified. But a corporation need not have such a legendary figure or storied history to perform effectively. That's fortunate. Otherwise, most companies would have to write off their futures.

By committing to a new design and an actual change agenda *in tandem* with a mission statement, the organization can minimize the likelihood that its words will ring hollow. This kind of multiple commitment represents a third trajectory, in which as much as possible, *intention and action are expressed simultaneously, not sequentially*.

THREE ROLES
FOR THE MANAGEMENT TEAM

The management team should play three overlapping roles in planning and managing the change process. First, the team should serve as an organizational *architect* in setting the direction for the entire organization; in sports terms, management must have the global perspective of a football head coach. The team's second role is to be an *exemplar* for the rest of the organization; as a group it should mirror the behaviors that it wishes to see exhibited throughout. In a sense the team must resemble a star baseball player whom the other players (individuals and organizational units) want to emulate. Third, the management team should be a *collaborator*. It is not enough for it to provide direction and set an example. Management must actually involve itself with other levels and parts of the organization. Metaphorically, the team should be the equivalent of a player-coach in basketball.

In fact, in assessing the current organization and conceptualizing the desired organization, the management team will already have played the role of architect—and to an extent, perhaps, that of collaborator. Now, in translating its vision into action, management must play all three roles. Of course, the degree to which the management team should play each role will vary with the nature of the desired organization. If this organization is control-based—a vertically-integrated firm, for instance—then the architect role will assume major importance, since the core management task is meshing the actions of many tightly linked organizational parts.

If the desired organization is autonomy-based—a widely dispersed conglomerate, for example—then management may need to stress the exemplar role since (1) the team's architect role will be limited to the design of a system in which units can be self-managing, and (2) its collaborator role will be limited by geography and by the diversity of the various businesses. (The more diverse and complex these businesses are, the more difficult it is for corporate managers to collaborate with their subordinates in problem-solving.)

If the desired organization is cooperation-based, featuring considerable horizontal integration, then by definition, the team's collaborator role will be pivotal. More so than with the other types of desired organization, architecture will be an ongoing task shared with others in the company. And while the management team's exemplar role remains important, this team cannot afford to operate from a distance to the degree that the team leading an autonomy-based organization can, but rather must continuously interact with the rest of the organization.

What we have in terms of the three team roles is still another instance of the need to blend universal and situational management principles. All management teams need to demonstrate all three roles; the relative importance of each, however, will depend on the nature of the desired organization.

Management as Architect

With a portrait of the desired organization in hand, the question becomes, How ready is your team to make it happen? You should test your resolve by estimating a time frame and the level of resources required. Resources consist chiefly of time, money, information, skills, and emotional energy. "Time," like the other resources, refers not just to the time of abstract others in the organization but also to the time your team itself will devote. This is where the rubber meets the road. Management not only must commit the organization to behavioral change; it must commit itself.

If there is a difference of opinion over the most appropriate generic change trajectory—for instance, multiple transitions versus one-step transformation—then you should consider the pros and cons of each. As with the exercise for conceptualizing the desired organization (Chapter 6), it may be helpful to sketch two or three alternatives and allow these to compete and "co-mingle" over a period of several weeks or if necessary, months. However long it may take, team members need to coalesce around a common design and route before sharing this vision with the rest of the organization.

The issue of time frame is in many cases problematic.

Depending on which management primer one reads, the appropriate change horizon may range from six months to a generation. Of course, it is always hazardous to venture general numbers because each case is so idiosyncratic, but here are some crude guidelines:

If the desired change constitutes no more than an adjustment, one year or less may be adequate. If you elect to embark on an organizational transition, then a one- to three-year horizon may be required; if a sequence of transitions, about two years for each may be realistic. One-step transformation? This one is especially problematic. I have been directly involved with several adjustments and (multiple) transitions, but never with what I would call a transformation. My best guess is that such a metamorphosis demands more time than a transition, but less time than would be the case if the process were partitioned into multiple transitions.

After working through these overarching change issues, your team needs to address specifics. How far should you go with any particular dimension on the Teamwork Profile? More basically, which dimensions are crucial? I have yet to work with a management team at any level that has explicitly mapped actions against every dimension early on. Rather, the tendency is to focus on a few "hot buttons" and address the other dimensions in terms of these.

Some of the best advice I know of for laying out a change agenda is that given by P. G. Herbst, the Norwegian behavioral scientist. Herbst advocates the design principle of "minimal critical specification."[2] The idea here is initially to define only the critical system or change parameters—those areas that have to be established at the start. By leaving other, noncritical aspects open, the organization has the opportunity to learn and adapt to unforeseeable conditions. To the extent that the management team follows Herbst's concept, it permits the rest of the organization some architectural initiative of its own.

Assume that your team wants to increase *cooperation* throughout the organization. Below are examples of broad "architectural" specifications that match the ten dimensions of the Teamwork Profile:

- Emphasize innovation/flexibility relative to cost/volume (distinctive competence).

- Supplement core internal capabilities with joint ventures and the selective use of consultants (developmental pattern).

- Encourage back-and-forth exchanges across functions and business units (coordinating mechanism).

- Err on the side of too much collaboration rather than too little (decision system).

- Circulate weekly performance results across divisions (information system).

- Link pay to group and organizational performance (reward system).

- Locate staff support offices right alongside the production process (effect of physical configuration).

- Expect people to make a special effort to help others when needed (organizational expectation).

- Minimize status symbols that separate people into one-up or one-down categories (individual expectation).

- Work toward solutions that incorporate, and blend, multiple perspectives (cultural bias).

Specifications may, of course, range beyond the dimensions laid out in the Teamwork Profile. For instance,

• Never sacrifice the long-term for short-term gains.

• Be driven by customer needs, not internal capacity.

• Build "bench strength" at all levels; make people development a high priority for every manager.

• Rely on shared values rather than dollars ("the carrot") or rules ("the stick") to guide behavior.

A contrasting but related perspective to Herbst's minimal critical specification is Gareth Morgan's provocative notion that instead of pursuing goals, organizations should concentrate on avoiding noxiants—negatives, things that are bad. By doing so, Morgan argues, they will increase their flexibility:

> a strategy based on the avoidance of noxiants involves a choice of limits and constraints rather than a choice of ends, creating degrees of freedom that allow meaningful direction to emerge. This cybernetic principle underlies many aspects of social life. It is no coincidence that most of our great codes of behavior are framed in terms of "thou shalt *not*." Whether we examine the Ten Commandments or contemporary legal systems, we find the principles of avoiding noxiants defining a space of acceptable behaviors within which individuals can self-organize. As new noxiants are identified, or old ones deemed less of a threat, they are typically added to or removed from the list, thus modifying the space of action in an evolving manner. Cybernetics suggests that this basic principle

could be usefully applied to help organizations learn
and evolve, and to help reduce the environmental tur-
bulence with which they have to deal.[3]

Actually, Herbst and Morgan are advocating complementary approaches. The first tack rules certain things in; the
second rules things out. (The difference is not unlike that
between basic types of homeowner and commercial insurance
policies. So-called "broad-form" policies detail what contin-
gencies *are* covered; "all-risk" policies specify what is *not*
covered.) Both approaches, however, have to do with minimal critical specification. Your team can benefit from combining them.

One important variant on minimal critical specification
concerns the sequencing of change activities. In my experience, the order of things does not much matter. I realize that
various writers have argued that some activities must come
early and others late. But I know of no practical or theoretical justification for *any* necessary sequence. In fact, in 14
years of organizational consulting I have never worked with
two organizations or teams that have ever followed the same
route—or in my view, *should* have followed the same route.

For some organizations it makes eminently good sense to
begin with "softening-up" activities related to organizational style. For other organizations, however, leading off
with things soft would be the kiss of death to any hopes for
a sustained change process. Moreover, the usual—and
healthy—pattern is to revisit earlier change activities in light
of more recent learning, so that the process takes on as much
a circular as a linear character.

Conceptually, the sequencing of change should be viewed
more as a mathematical *combination* than a *permutation*. In
a permutation, the elements of a set are arranged in a particular order. In a combination, by contrast, order is irrelevant;

all that matters is that all elements are included (and integrated). By minimizing unnecessary constraints on sequence, management maximizes its degrees of freedom. It also doesn't matter which comes first—mission or organizational design.

Two things do matter, however. First, the organization should start with problems or conditions or opportunities that it has energy around. People's desire to work on a particular issue or dimension is more important than any stylized notion of what logically should occur when. Second, mission and organizational design—and the various dimensions that make up design—eventually must get worked through in light of each other.

As we saw in Chapter 5, there are no hard and fast boundaries between mission and design, nor among the components of design—organizational strategy, structure, and style. Although it would probably be naive to address all design aspects in equal measure at the same time, it would also be a mistake to adopt a "Tinkertoy" mentality that seeks to make neat, discrete changes first to this component, second to that component, and so on—as if the components were modular. Christopher Alexander's description of how living systems develop certainly applies to organizations: "Structure is injected into the whole by operating on the whole and crinkling it, not by adding little parts to one another. In the process of differentiation, the whole gives birth to its parts: the parts appear as folds in a cloth of three-dimensional space which is gradually crinkled. The form of the whole, and the parts, come into being simultaneously."[4] To sum up the process: systemic, yes; lock-step, no.

Management as Exemplar

It is not enough for the management team to play a design role; team members must model those behaviors—and changes—that they advocate for the organization as a whole. As Bill Marriott, chairman of Marriott Corporation, has admitted, "If I sit back and relax, a lot of other people will sit back and relax. After all, if you're going to be a star performer, you can't sit back and relax. A star performer has to work hard and make sacrifices, and at Marriott Corp., we do both."[5] Honeywell CEO Edson W. Spencer has put the matter as follows: "The way the chief executive and senior managers of the company conduct themselves as individuals has a more profound impact on how other people in the company conduct *themselves* than anything else that happens."[6]

I believe that management's *team* behavior is no less important than its members' individual behavior. To some degree, your team should be a microcosm of the whole organization, especially if it is committed to furthering voluntary cooperation within and across different units and levels. In fact, published statements of mission, purpose, principles, and shared values may do more harm than good if the words serve simply to spotlight hypocrisy. Thus many companies over the last several years, in an honest attempt to point themselves in the right value direction, may have inadvertently set themselves up for abuse by underestimating the behavioral changes necessary to live the language.

This vulnerability exists as much at the facility level as at the corporate. Years ago, I worked with a labor-management committee in a factory with a sorry record of labor relations. Cooperative principles notwithstanding, the more time I spent with this joint committee, the more it became apparent that the thorniest problems lay within management, not between management and the union/workers. The union knew this. As the local president suggested at one point—after a meeting in which management representatives repeatedly tried to one-up each other—"I think you're spending your time with the wrong bunch. It's those guys [the plant's senior management team] who really need to be straight with each other and work together.''

The management team needs to think through its espoused values and then identify individual and collective behaviors that require change in order to match these values. Given the complexity of managing a modern corporation, the team obviously must know how to play all three games—in the same way that its leader must. In fact, it is fair to say that the team leader is to the team as the team is to the larger organization. Thus, Meredith Belbin in his book *Management Teams* describes an ideal team chairman as embodying ''skill in consultation [cooperation], delegation of work [autonomy], and firmness of decisions [control].''[7]

But while the management team, like its leader, requires versatility, it also needs a sense of game priorities. The Teamwork Profile is useful here. Below are examples, following the Profile, of the kind of concerns—and responses—that the management team might consider, assuming that it wants to reinforce change in the direction of greater *cooperation* among team members. (Needless to say, the Profile is equally helpful in moving towards greater autonomy of members and/or control over them.)

The team should be clear about *its* distinctive competence, not just that of the larger organization. The team might usefully ask itself what it does as a team that is truly innovative. The next question, of course, is what additional or different things it might do to become more innovative. Probably the best index of innovative activity is the team's agenda—how it spends its time. A move toward greater cooperation would be signaled by making innovation—through combining team members' own resources in untried ways—a more serious concern of these individuals.

What is the team's developmental pattern? How does it learn and renew itself? This question may be answered in part by specifying the degree to which the team interacts with others outside the organization—academics, consultants, peer managers, and so on. Cooperation in this connection means a readiness to "co-produce" outcomes with others, rather than to try to be self-sufficient.

The management team must coordinate itself as well as the organizational units for which it is responsible. There is no way that the team can function cooperatively without being in touch relatively frequently, whether or not in person. But the key is, what effort does each team member really make to ensure that his or her actions are coordinated with those of other team members? When they are not together, do team members naturally keep each other in mind? How strong an ethos is there of mutual adjustment—that is, of relying on informal, voluntary processes to coordinate activities?

The rest of the organization will take careful note of the team's decision system, which goes hand-in-hand with its internal coordinating mechanism. Cooperation implies a strongly consensual process within management. Although certain decisions will continue to be mandated by the team leader and other decisions will be delegated to individual team members, the overall pattern, if cooperative, will involve considerable sharing of authority. I know of no more effective means to understand and change the decision system than decision analysis (as discussed in Chapter 4).

What kind of information system does the team have? This question can be answered by mapping communication flows among team members. One-way trajectories and one-on-one patterns are not symptomatic of a distributed system. Sometimes the best evidence of a distributed system is the presence of charts, graphs, and other visual representations of important information that serve as a focal point for team members' interaction. In fact, the creation of such materials where none had existed before can by itself be a powerful spur to information-sharing. Graphic displays provoke reactions by—and exchanges among—those who view them.

A mutualistic reward structure has two features. First, the spread between highest and lowest members, or between levels, is not extreme. In Peter Drucker's terms, this means that the salary of the CEO, for instance, would not exceed by more than 30 percent those at a level below him or her.[8] Second, mutualistic rewards include a group component that reflects overall team and/or organizational performance. Beyond checking out these two features of their reward structure, the team might ponder just how much this structure does—and should—bring them together.

Where are team members "based," and in what ways do they interact? Spontaneous interaction requires more than that individuals have offices near each other. As Fritz Steele has pointed out, the typical "executive row" (and concomitant absence of a central meeting place) not only promotes stereotyped, nonspontaneous interactions; it also leads to compartmentalized thinking—by those who effectively reside in compartments.[9] Contrast this pattern with that of Citicorp under chairman John Reed. Reports *Forbes*:

> Symbolically, he sits on the second floor of the Citicorp headquarters on Park Avenue, not in the 15th-floor aerie used by [ex-chairman Walter] Wriston. Reed's front and back office walls are glass, so that passersby can watch the boss at work. His own office is nearly identical to ten others on the floor, each facing an indoor garden. The arrangement is intended to foster accessibility, a collegial atmosphere. In this office arrangement, Reed seems to be saying: No single person can run this show; the chief must rule by example and by inspiration.[10]

Every team can easily chart its own interaction patterns and relate these to its office configuration. As Steele shows, even dispersed managers can increase their spontaneous interaction by maintaining two (small) offices—one in the executive area and the other in the organizational unit or function for which they are responsible.

Members of the management team should be clear about what the team expects of them. If a high degree of collaboration is sought, then each individual must assume some responsibility for facilitating team functioning. Meredith Belbin describes this behavioral quality as "teamsmanship"—a very different mode from "gamesmanship," which amounts to one-upmanship. Teamsmen (teamspersons), according to Belbin, "have an ability to time their interventions, to vary their role, to limit their contributions, to create roles for others, and to do some of the jobs that others deliberately avoid."[11]

The complement of team expectation is member expectation. Collaboration requires and reinforces a sense of community. This means an absence of backbiting, of hidden agendas and political posturing. In a word, it means chemistry. This is precisely the quality that Reginald Jones put such stock in when he engineered his succession as chairman of General Electric.

Jones's famous "airplane interviews" were intended in large part to assess the chemistries of different combinations at the top. He put the following dilemma to potential successors: "You and I are in an airplane; it goes down, and neither of us survives. Who should be the next CEO?" Three months later, Jones confronted each candidate with a follow-up question: "I don't make it but you do. Now whom do you pick? And who else should be in the Corporate Executive Office?"[12]

Finally, an exemplary team that is committed to greater

cooperation needs to understand and strengthen member complementarity. The more complex and technology-based the organization, the greater the likelihood that team members' knowledge will not strongly overlap (except perhaps for financial and legal skills in a holding company). No one can know everything about everything. The need then is to find ways to blend the divergent skills—and perspectives—of team members so that team performance will exceed the sum of individual member contributions.

Management as Collaborator

Management-as-architect and management-as-exemplar are necessary for effective change, but they are not sufficient. The third, and perhaps most problematic, role for the team is to collaborate with the rest of its organization. This role is difficult in part because fulfilling the other two roles may actually distance management from the body of the organization. There is necessarily a top-down, one-way quality to the role of architect or designer, regardless of how many details are left for others to fill in. At the same time, the more the management team models desired behaviors—that is, the more cohesive and effective it becomes—the more it may actually seal itself off from the organizational levels below it. In one medium-sized firm that I have observed, the senior management team became so enamored of its newly developed ability to function consensually that it lost interest in—and contact with—the rest of the organization. It became a top, spinning atop the pyramid.

Examples of management teams' becoming cut off from the rest of the organization are legion. One of the most publicized cases is NASA, which after the *Challenger* tragedy in 1986 came under close scrutiny. In one post-mortem, *For-*

tune concluded that "The people at the top ended up isolated, a grimly instructive example of a problem that can
overtake any organization, governmental or corporate. . . .
The result: an organization in which the flow of vital information up and down was as flawed as the now-notorious
O-rings—the large synthetic rubber rings that were supposed
to seal the joints between the stacked sections of the solid-
fueled booster rockets."[13]

Just as the Teamwork Profile provides a useful organizing framework for the team's architect and exemplar roles,
so can this device help the team assess its role as collaborator.
Indeed, since the collaborator role is virtually synonymous
with the "cooperation" column on the Profile, the 10 Profile
dimensions can be viewed as a checklist. The discussion that
follows assumes that the team wants to increase voluntary
cooperation between itself and the rest of the organization.

In terms of distinctive competence, management needs to
explore the ways in which it has—or has not—teamed up
with unusual combinations of people from various levels and
units. How creative has management been in directly engaging the organization's resources? In what areas has the most
effort been expended? The least? Alternatively, where does
the most potential lie?

Developmental pattern will normally parallel distinctive
competence: A team that successfully innovates should be
comfortable working in concert with diverse individuals (and
groups) from outside the team. This means, above all, that
the boundary between management and nonmanagement is
permeable. People from both sides routinely cross it. A direct
way to gauge permeability is to recap what "outsiders" have
taken part in team meetings over, say, the past year. The flip
side is to track the visiting patterns of team members. Wal-
Mart, for instance, has institutionalized a practice in which
senior managers interact with employees by working in an

hourly position alongside them in a store for one week each year. Likewise, Disney executives spend a week at the parks selling food and collecting tickets. Delta Airlines' top managers meet with all employees, in groups, at least once every eighteen months.[14]

A "cooperative" coordinating mechanism relies on a lot of informal back-and-forth exchanges between the management team (and individual team members) and subordinate organizational levels/units. This pattern may be reinforced through the organization's formal decision system. A number of teams with which I am familiar have systematically analyzed the decisions for which they are responsible and then redesigned the decision-making process in a way that permits others deeper in their organizations to exercise influence. In one case, the senior team prepared a 13-page decision catalog and then progressively involved managers and professionals at other levels in critiquing and extending it. The decision system in this instance also served as a distributed information system. For the first time, people throughout the company came to understand clearly who had authority for what; they also were provided the opportunity to suggest improvements to the arrangement.

Speaking of information systems, consider what Southwestern Bell did just days after the AT&T breakup. According to Chairman and CEO Zane E. Barnes: "We viewed divestiture as a kind of emotional pressure point for people—and our research backed up this view. So right after divestiture, we staged a gigantic get-together that linked 55,000 employees and spouses in 57 locations via satellite. The objective was to provide a positive vent for divestiture-related emotions—an electronic catharsis, if you will. And we did, with visible leadership, hard business information, *and* old-fashioned fun, through humor, music, and dance. It was an unprecedented event for us which helped teach the power of shared emotional experiences and nontraditional media."[15]

The management team should assess its own reward structure in light of the reward structure for the rest of the organization. People's perceptions of equity are crucial, and perceived inequities may be expensive. General Motors learned (some would say, *should* have learned) this lesson the hard way in 1982 when, the same day that the United Auto Workers reluctantly agreed to $2.5 billion in long-term wage concessions, a new bonus scheme for top management was recommended to shareholders. The ill will generated by this faux pas helped blunt corporation-wide efforts to increase labor-management cooperation through quality-of-worklife programs.

In stark contrast to the General Motors caper stands the behavior of Nucor Corp., where percentage pay cuts—when they occur—increase with hierarchical standing. If a worker's pay is reduced by 25 percent, his department head's is likely to drop by 35 to 40 percent, and officers' pay may decline by 60 to 70 percent. CEO Ken Iverson says flatly, "Management should take the biggest drop in pay because they have the most responsibility."[16]

Physical configuration would seem to be an obvious thing to take into account in pursuing greater cooperation. All too often, however, this dimension is totally ignored. One index of executive remoteness: the metaphor that the rest of the organization uses to characterize senior managers' quarters. The crystal palace; Mecca; Mount Olympus; mahogany heaven. The more forbidding and inaccessible such quarters are, the less likely that the management team and others will collaborate.

A company that I observed several years ago provides a powerful lesson in how not to lay out an office if you want worker-manager cooperation. Overlooking the (first-floor) manufacturing area was a second-floor corner office whose glass walls gave managers a window on much of the production process. Managers would congregate in this nest and scrutinize the operation by quite literally looking down at the workers. While this arrangement saved management the hassle of frequently having to venture out onto the plant floor and interact personally, it also aroused resentment in the troops. The resentment, in turn, gave rise to a number of destructive games around a simple theme: let's see how much we can get away with in plain view! The workers got away with a lot.

If the organizational expectation is for collaboration, then such behavior had better take place *between* the management team and the rest of the organization—as well as within each. Honeywell president James J. Renier explains how his company has taken this principle to heart: "In setting the stage for our new corporate culture, we have been very careful to promote those managers who are comfortable in a participative milieu and to remove those who are not. This takes a lot of courage. You can't achieve an atmosphere of trust if anyone in the top management structure behaves in an inconsistent manner."[17]

One way in which the management team can reinforce a sense of community—that we're all on the same team and in this thing together—is to show employees that their future with the company need not be limited to a particular product or program or technology. Hence, if a product life-cycle goes south or a skill base becomes obsolete, the incumbents—with management's help—may find other opportunities within the firm.

The managers of a declining-products business team with which I am familiar drafted the following policy statement:

We are committed to those employees whose job assignments are in support of this declining business. . . . Their careers [within the corporation] will not suffer or be jeopardized by the ultimate cessation of [the product line].

• To this end we will continue the development of our people;

• As the market declines, we will reallocate our resources to other, more strategic businesses.

A commitment to complementarity recognizes that brains and leadership do not reside exclusively at the top of the hierarchy. Rather, these qualities are widely distributed and the management team leverages its capacities by engaging them wherever possible. In fact, the more this team helps to bridge the organizational boundaries separating levels, divisions, functions, and locations, the more will organizational performance approach its potential.

INTEGRATING TEAMS . . . OF TEAMS

The issue of the management team's collaborating with the rest of the organization raises a more general concern: How are teams . . . of teams throughout the corporation to be integrated?[18] Such a concern is rarely dealt with in conventional team-building, which, as noted in Chapter 2, is concerned mainly with small-group dynamics. At most, team-building addresses intergroup relations. But developing common ground between two or three small groups is hardly equivalent to cohering an organization of thousands, or tens or even hundreds of thousands.

In pursuing the (never-ending) goal of integration, the management team combines its architect, exemplar, and collaborator roles. One of the first tasks is to share the new corporate mission/design with the larger organization. This is best done in a cascading manner, either by following the organization chart or by using a participative structure that emphasizes organizational overlaps (as will be discussed shortly). Either way, group meetings should be held to permit every individual the opportunity:

(1) To assess the practical importance of each aspect of the mission/organizational design to him or her personally;

(2) To evaluate the extent to which the organization is behaving in accordance with each aspect of the mission/organizational design;

(3) To recommend courses of action to bring organizational behavior more in line with the language.

People can use a simple A-B-C-D-F grading system for (1) and (2). In making change recommendations, it may be useful to ask for two categories of suggestion: those that require action/approval by management; and those that can be implemented directly by the individual, or by his or her unit. This process will generate additions to the management team's action agenda and at the same time require the team to (further) delineate decision authorities.

Your team must determine for itself how much detail to share at the outset. The guiding criteria should be (1) likely relevance to employees, and (2) the retention of flexibility. *Inappropriate* detail will bore people. Thus, for instance, arcane information about the financial structure of the firm's markets and industries (under the "Customer" component of mission) may be of little general interest and therefore, not worth communicating. *Inordinate* detail about intended changes will limit the downstream options of your team— and indeed, of the entire organization. Hence, in describing organizational redesign, you should seriously consider the principle of minimal critical specification, as discussed earlier in this chapter.

The overriding challenge for the management team is to stimulate people and units throughout the organization to relate their parts to the corporate whole. Ultimately it is to be hoped that everyone in the organization will come to embrace the values embodied in the new mission/organizational design. To this end, management needs to reinforce certain linkages. *First*, intermediate (internal) customers must be connected to final (external) customers in people's minds. Figure 7.1 presents alternative perceptions of the customer sequence.

Those in work group A must understand the entire chain, and their crucial part in it, if "final customer" is to be meaningful to them. Here is an area where sharing information is not only appropriate but essential.

Dun & Bradstreet understands this need. D&B is committed to providing its clients with objective credit information. At D&B, according to James Heskett, "employees universally recognize the importance of accuracy in financial and other information they compile and disseminate. By communicating its expectations, the company encourages careful work."[19]

Sometimes the information-sharing task requires just a few minutes' explanation. In a large chemical plant with which I'm familiar, workers groused about having to fill five-gallon pails—a major headache compared to the 55-gallon drums they had been used to. The requirement for pails had been abruptly laid on them without any reasons why. It

Figure 7.1. Alternative Perceptions of the Customer Sequence

a. Intermediate Chain

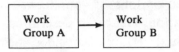

b. Extended Chain

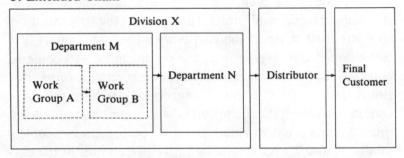

wasn't until a manager from outside their building explained, at an offsite meeting, the needs of the company's customers that the workers understood the importance of the pails. As this manager put it, "Our customers are insisting on this kind of convenience package, just as you insist on a five-pound bag of dog food for your puppy rather than a 50-pound bag." There was no problem from then on.

Second, unit and functional capabilities must be biased towards overall corporate capabilities. Every organization is made up of parts that have different objectives and performance criteria. For example, sales departments and basic R&D units historically have been autonomy-oriented; manufacturing operations tend to be control-based; and new-product application/commercialization groups are typically cooperation-oriented. These local perspectives are necessary, but they should be modified by the global perspective of the corporation—in the same way that intermediate customers should be reframed in terms of final customers. Thus, in a company that has committed itself to competing on the basis of innovation and flexibility, manufacturing and sales may retain their respective control and autonomy orientations yet simultaneously be biased towards the corporate mission. This dual focus means that local performance objectives—for example, maximizing equipment utilization or gross revenues—may have to be discounted for the sake of global performance that depends on voluntary coopertion. In effect, corporate priorities exert a sometimes countervailing influence on unit and functional priorities.

The integrative *processes* just discussed correspond to the three components of mission:

- Character (overarching values)

- Customers (intermediate: final)

- Capabilities (local: global)

There are also integrative *structures* that relate more directly to organizational design. Two structural approaches are common. The first type is situational and needs-driven. As an organization requires greater integration across functions or units, it implements increasingly powerful devices—ranging from individual liaison roles to more complex team and organizational designs.[20]

The second structural approach is based not on specific organizational needs but rather on general opportunities. Rensis Likert's "linking pin" organization, for instance, views the corporation as a set of overlapping groups that managers integrate vertically and laterally. According to Likert, this structure, when combined with shared decision-making, makes possible "an optimum integration of the needs and desires of the members of the organization, the shareholders, customers, suppliers, and others who have an interest in the enterprise or are served by it."[21]

A related structure that goes even further in developing overlaps among organizational units is Russell Ackoff's concept of planning teams and planning boards. Ackoff proposes making each unit of the organization a planning team, with virtually every team having a planning board—a structure that allows most managers to interact with as many as five levels of the organization.[22]

These alternative types of structural integration—situational versus general—parallel the familiar issue surrounding management principles: contingency versus universality (one-best-way). The "answer," of course, lies in a blending of the two perspectives.

Every organization has considerable choice in adopting integrative structures, just as it does in using integrative processes. One option that may hold particular promise is to use a participative structure like Ackoff's so that organizational parts can successively but interdependently define their own mission and team design, working from the senior team deeper and deeper into the company. This process would provide everyone with the kind of analytical experience that the top team had in crafting the corporate mission and design. At the same time it would help people relate their own capabilities and intermediate customers to those at the corporate level.

As a side benefit, the process can help sensitize managers to their own behavior in different contexts. For instance, in many large firms it is not uncommon for divisional general managers to enjoy a high degree of autonomy vis-à-vis their corporate bosses, but to grant precious little autonomy to their subordinates. Analogically, the GMs behave like baseball players looking up, but like football head coaches looking down. A systematic assessment/redesign process that features overlapping organizational levels can help reduce such inconsistency.

But perhaps the greatest potential value in extending the assessment/redesign process throughout the organization is the shared language that will develop. As Chapter 8 shows, the common use of a simple but powerful teamwork language can bind together the parts of a corporation in a way that transcends structure and process.

Integration Is Not Always the Answer

One disclaimer in all of the above: The assumption has been that organizational integration is positive and desirable, but such an assumption is not always valid. There are two generic classes of situation in which integration should be limited or even avoided. *First*, we have the case in which parts of the organization are dramatically different and have no need to interact—where, in fact, interaction may be harmful. Philip Selznick relates the story of Gar Wood, a boat-maker:

> The first boats made by Gar Wood were high-quality craft, made of the finest materials by master boat builders. Later, the company decided to mass-produce a comparatively low-cost speed-boat for wide distribution. It developed that the entire organization found itself unable to cope with the effort to shift commitments. Workmen and shop supervisors alike continued to be preoccupied with high-cost, quality craftsmanship. Members of the selling staff, too, could not shift emphasis from "snob appeal" to price appeal. The quality commitment was so strong that

an entirely new division—operating in a separate plant hundreds of miles away and therefore recruiting from a different labor market—had to be created to do the job successfully.[23]

A related case is the company that is simultaneously defending one set of products based on an old technology and attacking with another set of products based on a new technology. As Richard Foster has demonstrated, the strategic requirements of each set are so different that the organizational units involved ought not be mixed.[24]

The *second* generic class of situation where integration is problematic involves intentional internal competition among organizational units. The issue here is the extent to which the corporation should be viewed as a league versus a team. That issue will be treated in Chapter 8.

YOU ARE NEVER "THERE"

The title of this chapter, "Making It Happen," is misleading insofar as it implies finality. There is no such thing as once-and-for-all organizational change. Corporate players cannot redesign themselves and then expect to live happily ever after. Therein lies a major strength of the teamwork methodology: It is not an end-state in itself, but a means for shaping end-states—a framework that is infinitely reusable. The Teamwork Profile/Triangle can be particularly helpful as a guide to growing companies since organizational growth stages have distinct parallels with the different biases represented by autonomy, control, and cooperation.[25]

The one aspect of mission/design that ought to be relatively enduring, however, is organizational character. Although change may be the norm for products, markets, and industries—and for strategies, structures, and processes—a company cannot alter its fundamental character every few years. Should it try to do so, it will rob itself of character altogether.

Chapter Eight

A Teamwork Language for the Future

"The key to sailing is to be able to control your rudder, the weight of the boat, the position of the crew, and the sails. It's the combination of weight, sails, and rudder that steers the boat. The crew that does the best job controlling these three factors will usually win the race."

—GARY JOBSON, former *America's* Cup Champion[1]

Effective corporate teamwork, like sailing, also depends on three factors—autonomy, control, and cooperation. Taken together, these dimensions form a kaleidoscope within which any blend of teamwork can be created and recreated. They form a teamwork *language* that can guide organizational strategy, structure, and style.

The kind of organization that a corporation becomes is always a function of the teamwork language in use. If the language is simplistic, then the behavior that it spawns will not match the complexity the company confronts. Alternatively, if the language is dense, then it will not be widely used even if it is up to the task. The trick is to employ a language that is both powerful and understandable—and congenial.

As I suggested in Chapter 2, popular appreciations of teamwork and organizational design are deficient. "Teamwork" is typically equated with small-group dynamics, and it is indeed the rare organization that recognizes that there is more than one kind of teamwork—and team. For its part, organizational design remains narrowly construed as one- or two-dimensional—a never-never land of centralization versus decentralization. Logical connections between teamwork and organizational design are seldom drawn by managers.

Every organization is unique. In this respect, every organization is like a piece of nature. No two things in nature are ever identical. No two trees are precisely the same. Nor are any two sand pebbles or snowflakes. Indeed, as Christopher Alexander has pointed out, no two *atoms* are exactly alike.[2] But in every case in nature, variety occurs within a framework that is defined chiefly by a few critical dimensions. Uniqueness and universality go hand in hand.

Consider the snowflake. For all the septillions of octillions of flakes that have fallen to earth, no two have ever been (or will ever be) identical. Yet every flake is hexagonal or triangular—and symmetrical. Explains Charles Osgood:

"The reason they are symmetrical is that the water freezes into a six-sided crystal, but the varying forces of temperature, wind, and humidity and the pull of surface tension and escaping heat cause the magnificent lace-doily patterns we associate with snowflakes."[3] So what we have here is the interaction of a few "strategic" variables to produce a near-infinite variety of shapes within a stable set of patterns. The organizational design framework presented in this book has similar properties. This language offers a way to represent what is distinctive about an organization within a structure that applies to all organizations. Put somewhat differently, the teamwork language captures the particular in light of the general—the situational in light of the universal. In so doing, it demonstrates an uncommon degree of usability, flexibility, and robustness.

ADVANTAGES OF THE TEAMWORK LANGUAGE

To begin with, every organization—and every organizational unit—is already in the ballpark. That is, every organization is already inside the Teamwork Triangle since by definition an organization must blend autonomy, control, and cooperation. Hence, even transformation can be conceptualized as a reordering of current priorities rather than the invention of wholly new ones. This means that virtually every point of view inside the organization has legitimacy. For no matter how radical the change required, some measure of each of the three pulls will remain necessary. Contrast this approach to change with the more familiar binary perspective in which people and interests are either lined up for a new direction or dug in against it—in classic either/or, win/lose fashion.

Of course, none of the above is to say that wrenching changes will never be required—that no one will ever be hurt. But the three-dimensional language does transcend primitive, dichotomous thinking and recognizes that every point of view has some value. No outlook or attitude is completely "wrong," any more than another is completely "right."

Now for flexibility. At a rudimentary level, this language offers the choice between a detailed medium (the Teamwork Profile) and a broad-brush one (the Triangle)—or, of course, a combination of these. Either can play the lead role, which is another way of saying that either the nitty-gritty or the big picture can come first. At a deeper level, the choice has to do with the use of metaphor.

The teamwork language is grounded in the structure of actual sports teams. In using this framework, every organization has the option of emphasizing the sports-team likenesses or ignoring them. Different persons and organizations will have different stylistic preferences and different degrees of metaphorical fluency. The organizational design framework is flexible because it is compatible with just about any posture.

I have encountered three patterns of response to sports-team metaphors: reliance, acceptance, and avoidance. At one extreme, avoidance, managers are suspicious of metaphor in general and sports metaphors in particular. Such individuals are fond of claiming that "We don't play games around here!"—evoking Eric Berne's ironic category of playing "the game of not playing a game." As often as not, in the next breath there is an unselfconscious boast: "But our organization is clearly a winning team."

In the opposite pattern, reliance, managers embrace team sports as metaphors in large part because they and their company strongly identify with athletic competition. Some individuals will have played on organized teams in high school and college, while many others at least have been fans for much of their lives. The usefulness of sports metaphors in everyday business conversation is taken for granted. In such a setting, it is an easy next step from casually to systematically using expressions like "We've got too many baseball players around here" or "We need to pass the ball a lot more."

Between these extremes lies acceptance, an outlook that is neither partial to nor hostile to metaphorical thinking. Sports—and other—metaphors are interspersed throughout normal dialogue, and are used especially to reinforce particular points.

Actually these three perspectives are not so far apart as they may seem, if only because language and thought patterns are inherently metaphorical. It is impossible to speak or write or think nonmetaphorically, and those metaphors that we use routinely are the means by which we structure reality. There is also evidence that metaphor—which in effect means "word-picture"—is essential to creativity. Roger von Oech has observed that "much of creative thinking is visual in orientation. Indeed, a study of 100 leading mathematicians showed that they did their best work when they had images in their minds, not when they were thinking of mathematical symbols."[4]

The teamwork language is robust because it is at once metaphorical and empirical. This framework is more visually evocative than most empirically (or theoretically) derived schemes, and more practically applicable than most metaphorical schemes. Thus, at one extreme, organizations that wish to avoid references to baseball-football-basketball benefit from the implicit structure of the framework's grounding in team sports. At the other extreme, organizations relying on the sports metaphors can easily transfer to their own reality—a conversion that is difficult with most other metaphors.

For years, consultants have used metaphor as a way to help clients express their perceptions and feelings. A common technique is to ask individuals to characterize their organization in terms of a vehicle (mechanism) or an animal (organism). This exercise frees up people so that they can reveal critical opinions. A sampler:

> We're a muscle car. We're fast and flashy, and a lot of people look at us from the outside and admire what they see. But we're also expensive to operate and maintain, and we don't take the corners nearly as well as our international competitors—the BMWs, Porsches, Saabs. We're designed to go flat out on the straight away; just don't ask us to take on mountain roads.

> The parent corporation is a crocodile. It eats anything it can get to. Did you know that baby crocodiles, as soon as they break out of the egg, are snapping their jaws? It's all genetically coded in them. We're the same way. We're coded to gobble up anything we get near. To call this company a predator is to be charitable.

As provocative as descriptions like these are, the question remains: What do you do with them? It is tough to go from such a generalized portrait to practical implications—from the issue of "what?" to that of "so what?"—just because the metaphors are literally so different from organizational reality. The team-sports metaphors, by contrast, are close enough to corporate structures to permit meaningful comparison across several dimensions.

The best example I know of a company that is predisposed to using sports metaphors is Frito-Lay, Inc., a major division of highly competition-oriented PepsiCo, Inc.[5] Frito-Lay has "relied" on baseball, football, and basketball as organizational design models for conceptualizing a "model division" for the firm. The division is the primary unit into which Frito's 10,000-person sales force is organized; each of the 40 divisions consists of sales-persons, sales supervisors and managers at different levels, and various support staff.

Under the facilitation of management development specialists Abe Raab and Derek Wendelken, three groups of sales management personnel were assembled and charged with the following task: design the structure of an ideal division as if it were a baseball team (first group), a football team (second group), or a basketball team (third group). This process produced three highly detailed and divergent portraits of a Frito-Lay division, each with its distinctive strengths and weaknesses. The various models included such features as "bench support," "utility players," and "farm systems." Core business skills were matched with equivalent athletic skills. Organization structure was patterned after sports-team hierarchy: front office/general management, coaching staff, starting team, backup players.

Frito-Lay used the sports models in a manner similar to Synectics, Inc.'s concept of "excursion"—the generation of a metaphorical lens through which to view a phenomenon.[6] After the excursion into metaphor, the idea is to return to the presenting problem or objective (or organization) in more literal terms, but with fresh perspective. Frito-Lay followed just this route. The three sports models were compared and contrasted, and then integrated into a composite set of recommendations in nonsports language. It is likely that certain of these recommendations will be implemented.

Frito-Lay demonstrates how readily the three-dimensional design framework permits companies to draw out metaphor. Frito also illustrates another flexible property of this framework: its applicability to any unit of analysis. The redesign exercise discussed above took place within a multibillion-dollar entity that itself was changing from one kind of team into another. Charlie Feld, vice president of management services, places Frito's corporate shift in perspective:

> From 1968 through 1981, we enjoyed 15% to 20% annual revenue growth through geographic expansion, premium pricing, and major new accounts. We added 200 or 300 new sales routes a year, and it was all incremental business. In those days, we were capacity-constrained; we just couldn't build plants quickly enough. By 1981, we had built manufacturing into an awesome machine, but all of a sudden the marketplace changed and we had excess capacity. We needed a new configuration of the company—growth not through pricing and geographic expansion but through higher-risk new products and sales productivity in our existing geography. The concept was certainly right, but the linkage between the strategies and the execution takes time. *It's as if you had to get your championship football team to play basketball. You look around and find you have a lot of big guys still wearing helmets*. Fortunately we're coming out of it now. Our spirit will carry us through. [Emphasis added.][7]

A NEW CORPORATE DESIGN

Because the teamwork language can be applied to any unit of analysis, this framework can help to integrate organizations as people throughout gain a deeper appreciation of teamwork possibilities.[8] Regardless of how far metaphor is pursued—that is, whether the terms are baseball-football-basketball or autonomy-control-cooperation—everyone can come to speak the same language. A shared vocabulary will reduce the separative effects of hierarchy, geographical dispersion, and functional differences.

Awareness of organizational design options will, in many cases, spur interest in a new teamwork mix—one that places greater emphasis on voluntary cooperation. The process is paradoxical: By expanding their teamwork horizons—comprehending more alternatives and combinations than they ever had in the past—people come to realize the value of nurturing a particular form of teamwork throughout their organization.

The effect of this process is similar to that which follows reconceptualizing the organization as a hologram—a three-dimensional image in which each part is a microcosm of the whole. Gareth Morgan has explicated the parallels between the hologram and the brain as a basis for a new organizational design. The core principle is high (and highly flexible) connectivity among parts. Different regions of the brain specialize in different activities, but all are interdependent and capable of assuming one another's roles as necessary. Nerve cells (neurons) throughout the brain are richly connected to each other—a fact that permits different parts of the brain to process information in parallel and to know what is happening in other parts. Morgan suggests that by developing rich connectivity among their parts, organizations can increase both specialist and generalist skills, and their members' ability to reorganize: "The holographic principle has a great deal running in its favor. For the capacities of the brain are already distributed throughout modern organizations. All the employees have brains, and computers are in essence simulated brains. In this sense, important aspects of the whole are already embodied in the parts. The development of more holographic, brainlike forms of organization thus rests in the realization of a potential that already exists."[9]

The "ideal" holographic organization is a basketball team whose parts are interacting basketball teams, all of whose players have high "court-awareness." But that's an abstraction. Practically, every organization, including those that are playing baseball or football—metaphorically or literally—will feel the need for holographic qualities as learning and adaptability become ever more central to survival.

Note the parallel between Morgan's observation that the potential for this design already exists and my earlier statement (p. 185) that "every organization—and organizational unit—is already in the ballpark . . . already inside the Teamwork Triangle." The potential to reorganize in a way that reinforces voluntary cooperation is contained in the logic of the organizational design framework. As a result, to paraphrase Marshall McLuhan, the medium implies the message.

The new game for knowledge-based corporations will favor transition over possession, fluid positions over fixed, ball movement over ball control; in essence, change over continuity. These design criteria present no structural problems for the small firm. But for large corporations, or for growing companies that aspire to be large, a "basketball" design based on voluntary cooperation is problematic. It is simply unrealistic to rely on informal coordinating processes—everyone in touch with everyone else—when an organization (or indeed, a group) reaches a certain scale. The most appropriate design for large corporations that face dynamic environments is what I have referred to (in Chapter 6) as an autonomy/cooperation hybrid.

An *autonomy/cooperation hybrid* is made up of organizational units that (1) are relatively autonomous vis-à-vis corporate headquarters, (2) feature a blend of autonomy and voluntary cooperation with respect to each other, and (3) exhibit a high degree of voluntary cooperation internally. Contrast this design with the divisional structure that characterizes most Fortune 500 companies today. Divisionalization attempts to blend the advantages of centralization with those of decentralization through corporate policy setting and divisional operating freedom. In terms of the teamwork language, divisionalization produces a near-symmetrical mix of autonomy and control—an autonomy/control hybrid—especially to the extent that divisional management is authoritarian. The differences between the two hybrids are summarized in Table 8.1.

The divisional firm is the predictable product of a two-dimensional organizational design vocabulary. It is a sensible design for a stable world: one in which strategic thinking need reside only at the top, and where divisions can consume resources without regard for one another's needs—or the needs of their own people. Such a milieu is made to order for those who live by the puerile credo "Lead, follow, or get out of the way." In a turbulent world whose every day is "crunch time," however, this design cannot deliver. Initiative, intelli-

Table 8.1   CONTRASTING ORGANIZATIONAL HYBRIDS

	THE FAMILIAR DIVISIONAL DESIGN: AUTONOMY/CONTROL HYBRID	A NEW CORPORATE DESIGN: AUTONOMY/ COOPERATION HYBRID
Dominant unit: corporation relation(s)	Autonomy and control	Autonomy
Dominant unit: unit relation(s)	Autonomy	Autonomy and cooperation
Dominant intra-unit relation	Control	Cooperation

gence, and imagination are needed throughout the organization—up, down, and across.

To be sure, there will continue to be firms that are effectively structured as autonomy/control hybrids; McDonald's and several other franchise-based companies are prominent examples. There will also continue to be viable control/cooperation hybrids—"humanistic hierarchies." Many enlightened manufacturers, (nuclear) energy producers, and service firms (such as airline companies)—all with special control and/or safety requirements—will fit this description. But the information-based corporation of the future will, I believe, correspond most closely to a blend of autonomy and cooperation.

Now for matrix organization. As I indicated in Chapter 2, matrix designs implicitly try to get the best of all three worlds—autonomy, control, and cooperation—even though their proponents believe they are pursuing only two worlds. In fact, the customary logic for matrix organization is quite similar to that for divisionalization: combining autonomy (local responsiveness and focus through a product/market emphasis) and control (global perspective and consistency/efficiency through a functional emphasis). But matrix organizations cannot operate without some measure of voluntary cooperation, even if this dimension remains subordinate—or unconscious. Divisionalized corporations, by contrast, historically have been able to operate without much cooperation among divisions.

Corporations that have experimented widely with matrix designs may find it easier to move toward an autonomy/cooperation hybrid than firms without such experience. Matrix demands generalist thinking throughout the organization—taking into account multiple viewpoints, making frequent trade-offs. It also requires a high managerial tolerance for ambiguity and a large measure of spontaneous cooperation. Such qualities are not requisites in the classical division-alized culture, where divisional autonomy is inviolate. Emerson Electric is a good example of the challenge facing an autonomy/control hybrid that seeks to increase interdivisional sharing of resources in order to become more high-technology oriented. Observed *Business Week* in 1983: "Several Emerson insiders suggest that the battle to change Emerson's old culture is far from won. Some division presidents openly acknowledge that they are wary about compromising their autonomy by cooperating with their peers."[10]

In any case, the two primary routes to an autonomy/cooperation hybrid are sketched in Figure 8.1. Matrix may or may not be a stepping stone.

The autonomy/cooperation hybrid is similar to what Harvard's Michael Porter has dubbed a "new organizational form," an amalgam of autonomy and interrelationships.[11] Prominent examples are 3M, NEC, Hewlett-Packard, Gore Associates, American Express, and Saab-Scania. Since 1982, American Express chairman and CEO James D. Robinson has made inter-unit collaboration a high priority. Robinson's "One Enterprise" initiative requires senior managers to specify in their strategic plans concrete opportunities for voluntary cooperation across the firm. Managers and professionals are evaluated on the basis of their cooperative behavior. According to Amex's 1986 annual report, operating units are expected to capitalize on "opportunities inherent in their complementary strengths in markets, product lines and cultures. Through joint projects—sharing data-processing technology, marketing expertise and staff, as well as cross-selling products and services—our businesses have succeeded in compounding their individual capabilities to meet their customers' needs. So far, we have initiated some 260 One Enterprise projects, the vast majority of which have yielded more productive use of the Company's resources and an enhancement of bottom-line results."

Figure 8.1. The Evolution of Complex Corporate Design

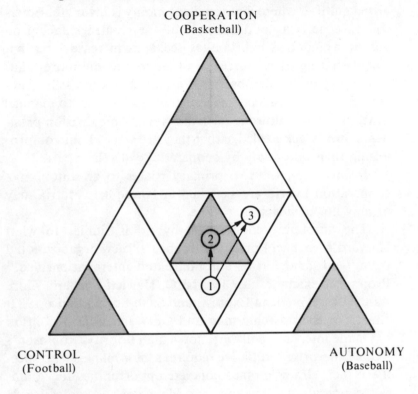

COOPERATION
(Basketball)

CONTROL
(Football)

AUTONOMY
(Baseball)

Legend:　① Divisional Structure

　　　　　② Matrix Organization

　　　　　③ Autonomy/Cooperation Hybrid

Saab-Scania's purpose is "moving people and goods efficiently, whether in cars, trucks, buses or aircraft."[12] Considerable idea-sharing takes place among divisions. Saab's 900 and 9000 series automobiles, for instance, incorporate instrument, soundproofing, climate control, and seat design features that are the result of research done by the Saab Aircraft division. The Scania division's experience in turbocharging diesel engines for trucks and buses has been transferred to the car engines that Scania also builds.

From a conceptual standpoint, the autonomy/cooperation hybrid reflects what may be the dominant production thrust of the last decade: the compression of long-linked sequences (a development that mirrors, and benefits from, parallel-processing computers). With this trend have come several new organizational features, including a lessened reliance on top-down coordination, a reduction in hierarchical levels, a reduction in job classifications, and decision processes that involve more people simultaneously—rather than sequentially—than ever before. Mostly, such changes have been in the name of responsiveness, flexibility, quality, and creativity—a departure from yesterday's economies-of-scale religion. Manufacturing expert Ramchandran Jaikumar describes what this shift means for industrial organization:

> What, after all, is a manufacturing company? Today, no artist would represent a factory as a huge, austere building with bellowing smokestacks. The behemoth is gone. The efficient factory is now an aggregation of small cells of electronically linked and controlled FMSs [flexible manufacturing systems]. New technology enables these operating cells to be combined in nonlinear ways. No shared base of infrastructure mandates large-scale production integration. The days of [Frederick] Taylor's immense, linear production systems are largely gone.[13]

In informational terms, the contrast can be summed up as the difference between writing a book on a word processor and writing it on a typewriter. To write a book on a typewriter usually requires significant up-front outlining—especially if the subject is technical. Much of the thinking-through process has to take place before any prose is created, for one overriding reason: changes are notoriously difficult to make. Adding or deleting or modifying a few sentences could make it necessary to retype the entire document. For practical purposes, the writer has to get things right from the start.

When using a word processor, the writer is able to combine outlining and writing—planning and doing. He or she can outline as the book develops. Because changes can be implemented effortlessly, there is no need to get it all laid out at the outset. One can make changes anywhere and of any length, and can produce endless drafts with minimal inconvenience. But more important than these efficiency savings is the gain in effectiveness that word processing brings about.

The act of writing becomes a much richer learning experience because the writer can interact with the entire document at any point in its construction. He can have a dialogue with himself and his thoughts in a way that is impossible when a typewriter is used. Karl Weick sums up the process by which people make sense of organizational reality with the question "How can I know what I think until I see what I say?"[14] The idea is that retrospection is vital to self-awareness and understanding. Word processing offers the writer exactly this opportunity—to see what he has said, and therefore thinks, in a way that can be readily restated.

The old typing—or indeed, handwriting—method carried with it heavy demands for a priori reasoning. It represented a "brilliant game plan" model in which detailed initial planning was crucial. In contrast, word processing reflects the design concept of minimal critical specification (as described in Chapter 7); the technology permits one to plan as he or she goes. Word processing enables one to transform the writing task from a narrowly linear, sequential process into one that is also circular and reciprocal. It recalls the breakthrough that William Bernbach provoked in creative advertising when he converted the traditional, serial copywriter-to-artist process into a dynamic back-and-forth exchange between these players.

A LEAGUE OR A TEAM?

From a human-resources standpoint, the key behavioral characteristic of the autonomy/cooperation hybrid is its emphasis on independence and interdependence relative to dependence. People are expected to take responsibility for managing their own jobs and careers and, at the same time, to look for ways in which they can add value by voluntarily helping others throughout the company. These expectations mean a departure from bureaucratic principles in which boundaries among functions, and between functional and product/market perspectives, are impermeable. Hierarchical boundaries also need to be minimized—especially those separating managers and workers. In 1986, deputy Under Secretary of Labor Steven I. Schlossberg argued that "for the last 50 years, the law has assumed that labor and management are adversarial opponents and must have an arms-length relationship. If we're going to be competitive in the global economy, we may have to blur distinctions between labor and management."[15]

At a structural level, the independence/interdependence combination raises the issue of the extent to which the organization should be viewed as a "league" versus a team (. . . of teams). A league atmosphere can energize corporate units and individuals and instill a healthy competitive spirit—as seems to have happened at such companies as Citicorp, Procter & Gamble, PepsiCo, General Electric, and ADP. It can also provide an intermediate organizational system that people can readily identify with and feel able to influence—no small advantage in a multibillion-dollar corporation. Taken too far, however, the league concept can understate interdependence and undermine any sense of corporate unity—as may be the case when players compete more fiercely against their internal counterparts than against external competitors.

The autonomy/cooperation hybrid must strike an especially delicate balance. The players in this kind of organization must be able both to compete and to collaborate—and to know when to do which. In this regard, corporations might take a cue from some of the organizational consultants that they employ. It is the norm for many consultants (including myself) to compete with their peers (for clients or projects) in certain situations and to collaborate closely in other situations. Such paradoxical behavior is a requirement for survival, given the ever-changing terrain that consultants must negotiate. But consultants—at least, many of them—are either soloists or members of a small-scale organization. Corporations, by contrast, are made up of people who have a stake in the performance of an organization that is considerably larger than themselves. To this extent, any "league" component that encourages internal competition must be tempered by shared commitment to an overarching corporate mission.

In the opposite direction, however, the consultant analogy has further value: It demonstrates the importance of collaborating with others outside as well as inside the corporation. Historically, American companies have gone to great lengths to remain self-sufficient. This kind of mentality no longer works. Instead, complementary relationships with others—including suppliers, customers, sometime competitors, government, and academe—are taking on increasing importance. The realization is dawning that going it alone may be more risky than teaming up. Such is nowhere more the case than in scientific research, given the rapid obsolescence of knowledge. Predicted White House science adviser George A. Keyworth II in 1985: Collaborative research [between business and universities] "is going to be the driving force for 21st-century industrial technology."[16]

TEAMWORK
BEYOND THE CORPORATION

The teamwork language in this book is applicable to any organizational unit of analysis—and, I believe, to any type of social system. Although my focus has been on corporate players, there is no reason that these concepts cannot be applied in other sectors, including government, education, and the military. In fact, one can characterize such disparate systems as the family and the nation-state in terms of a blend of autonomy, control, and cooperation.

The traditional American family has been control-oriented. Whether the model is benign (*Father Knows Best*) or less than benign (*The Great Santini*), father and his career clearly come first. In effect, he calls the shots for everyone else. Mother's role is separate from and subordinate to father's; her task is to manage the household and bring up the children. The latter make up the bottom of the three-tiered family hierarchy and are in an absolutely dependent position vis-à-vis their parents—especially father.

Perhaps the most familiar example of an autonomy-oriented family is the modern, dual-career couple in which mother's career is more or less on a par with father's. Each does his/her own thing without any hierarchical ordering separating them. Children are likewise on their own—at least relative to their counterparts in a control-based family. An extreme case of the autonomy-oriented family is the "dink" couple—*d*ouble-*i*ncome, *n*o-*k*ids—in which husband and wife see each other chiefly at the airport, as each follows a career trajectory that is independent spatially as well as substantively.

A cooperation-oriented family features minimal hierarchy and minimal segmentation of roles. Father and mother (husband and wife) have overlapping careers. At the least, this means that each seeks guidance and counsel from the other. But it may also mean that the partners actually share a job or collaborate professionally as a pair. In any case, just as their work is shared, so are household and child-rearing responsibilities. For their part, children in a cooperation-oriented family have a greater voice than those in a control-based family; they are also "closer" to their parents' work than are kids in an autonomy-based family.

Now consider nations. For the sake of illustration, consider these three: the United States, the Soviet Union, and Japan. Can anyone doubt that the United States is an autonomy-oriented society? After all, our roots are in the wide open spaces of the frontier—and in its economic equivalent: unfettered, free-market capitalism. Our private and public sectors have remained apart—independent societal players as it were. Recent trends towards deregulation and privatization have only reinforced this tendency. It is hardly any wonder that our "national pastime" is baseball.

Few would question that the Soviet Union is a control-oriented society, centrally planned and managed. That nation resembles a mammoth bureaucracy in which individual and organizational roles are highly specified and constrained—both by the rules built into the system and by the administrators who operate it. There is no private sector to speak of; productive organizations are a subset of the state.

Japan is cooperation-oriented, although this cast is tempered by an implicit, abiding presence of control—a post-feudal legacy. Many observers believe that deeply ingrained patterns of voluntary cooperation have been essential to Japan's survival. While more than twelve times as densely populated as the United States, that nation has virtually no natural resources. Hence, the Japanese either use their ingenuity and commitment in harmony, or they collectively sink into the ocean. This imperative has translated into signal collaboration between managers and workers, between firms, between financial and goods-producing enterprises, and between private and public sectors. (In light of such patterns, a continuing anomaly in Japan is the highly control-based family structure, in which women play a decidedly inferior role.)

In my own view, the United States needs to move in the direction of increased societal cooperation—public–private–academic, private–private, labor–management. Japan, by contrast, may do well to encourage a greater sense of individual autonomy—both within and outside the work organization. The Soviet Union appears to have the greatest distance to travel in order to become a world-class economic player; its strong control orientation is a liability in an information era that defines success in terms of invention, flexibility, and adaptability. The beginnings of *glasnost*—"openness"—are a positive sign.

How does all of this relate to corporate players? In the case of Japan and the Soviet Union, the structure of productive organizations appears to mirror that of the larger society. To this extent, both corporations (and their economic equivalents) and the national cultures in which they are embedded need to move in the same general direction. In the United States, by contrast, the control bias of most corporations contrasts with our laissez-faire national culture. Hence, while society as a whole should place greater emphasis on voluntary cooperation—in effect holding control "constant"—many of our companies need to increase both cooperation and autonomy relative to control.

None of this is to suggest naively that the autonomy/cooperation hybrid is a kind of magic triangle to which every company—and every nation—should aspire. Although I believe that this blend does represent the large, dynamic corporation of the future, it certainly is not the only model. And it would indeed be ludicrous to argue that diverse countries should all aim for the same blend of priorities, as if deep cultural mores could be easily transmuted. On the other hand, there is every reason to believe that tomorrow will reward behavior that maximizes a blend of independence and interdependence and minimizes dependence. To that extent, the arrows indicated in Figure 8.2 may signify important directions.

Such movement is as essential among nations as it is among sectors and among corporations. Each day the world more closely approximates Marshall McLuhan's "global village." National players, like corporate players, need to be able to compete and to collaborate with each other simultaneously. When they are able to do so, such players will transcend the limitations of the sports-league concept—which is inherently zero-sum. They will form a different kind of league—a non-zero-sum covenant based on furthering mutual interests. As Princeton economist William Baumol has written, "Nations need not view one another as rivals in productivity growth. In the long run, each of us benefits from what the other achieves. Whatever encourages effective innovation in one country contributes to economic welfare in oth-

Figure 8.2. US, USSR, JAPAN: Contrasting Patterns
and Needed Directions

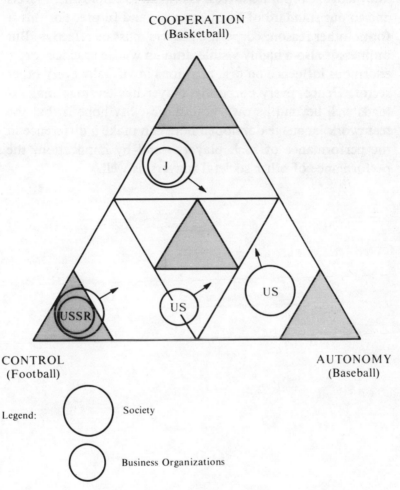

COOPERATION
(Basketball)

CONTROL
(Football)

AUTONOMY
(Baseball)

Legend: Society

               Business Organizations

ers. Competitiveness, viewed in this light, is primarily a
short-run issue."[17]

In many ways, business is the leading part of world society. Business organizations dominate the use of precious human and technological resources—and in turn, are the source

of a never-ending stream of new products, services, and knowledge. Corporate success is critical to employment levels and to our standard of living, current and future. For this if for no other reason, corporate players must be effective. But business is also a highly visible domain whose practices exert enormous influence on organizations in virtually every other sector. Hence, every corporate player has leverage that extends well beyond its own boundaries. My hope is that the teamwork language developed here can make a difference in the performance of such players—and by implication, the performance of other societal players as well.

Appendix

The three categories making up the organizational design framework—strategy, structure, and style—underlie much of the organizational assessment literature. The following matrix presents my impression of how ten representative assessment schemes match these categories—although it is clear that several of the dimensions could be placed under more than one heading.

ORGANIZATIONAL ASSESSMENT FRAMEWORKS IN TERMS OF ORGANIZATIONAL STRATEGY, STRUCTURE, AND STYLE

AUTHOR	ORGANIZATIONAL		STYLE	STRATEGY, STRUCTURE	STRATEGY, STYLE	STRUCTURE, STYLE	STRATEGY, STRUCTURE, STYLE	OTHER (OUTSIDE THE ORGANIZATION)
	STRATEGY	STRUCTURE						
Leavitt (1972)	Task	Structure Technology	People					The environment
Galbraith (1977)		Structure Reward system Information & decision processes		Task		People		
Kotter (1978)		Employees & other tangible assets			Dominant coalition	Key organizational processes		External environment

		Formal organizational arrangements					Social system		
	Strategy	Technology	Structure	Systems	Rewards	Style	Staff Skills	Superordinate goals*	Current economic climate
McKinsey & Co. (1979)	Strategy		Structure	Systems		Style	Staff Skills	Superordinate goals*	
Kanter (1983)	Strategy		Organization structure	Information flow	Rewards	Culture / Current "emotional" climate	Communication emphasis / Current change issues		Current economic climate
Tichy (1983)			Technical system			Cultural system	Political system		
Davis (1984)	Strategy					Culture			
Hickman & Silva (1984)	Strategy					Culture			

(cont.)

ORGANIZATIONAL ASSESSMENT FRAMEWORKS IN TERMS OF ORGANIZATIONAL STRATEGY, STRUCTURE, AND STYLE (Continued)

AUTHOR	ORGANIZATIONAL			STRATEGY, STRUCTURE	STRATEGY, STYLE	STRUCTURE, STYLE	STRATEGY, STRUCTURE, STYLE	OTHER (OUTSIDE THE ORGANIZATION)
	STRATEGY	STRUCTURE	STYLE					
Kilmann (1984)		Reward system	Culture Team-building	Strategy-structure	Management skills			
Quinn & Kimberly (1984)		Organizational form	Motivation leadership		Effectiveness values	Compliance	Decision-making	

*Later changed to "Shared Values"

References

Davis, Stanley M. 1984. *Managing Corporate Culture*. Cambridge, MA: Ballinger.

Galbraith, Jay R. 1977. *Organization Design*. Reading, MA: Addison-Wesley.

Hickman, Craig R., and Silva, Michael A. 1984. *Creating Excellence*. New York: New American Library.

Kanter, Rosabeth Moss. 1983. *The Change Masters: Innovation for Productivity in the American Corporation*. New York: Simon & Schuster.

Kilmann, Ralph H. 1984. *Beyond the Quick Fix: Managing Five Tracks to Organizational Success*. San Francisco: Jossey-Bass.

Kotter, John P. 1978. *Organizational Dynamics: Diagnosis and Intervention*. Reading, MA: Addison-Wesley.

Leavitt, Harold J. 1972. *Managerial Psychology* (2nd ed.). Chicago: University of Chicago.

McKinsey & Company, 1979. New York: *McKinsey Staff Paper*.

Quinn, Robert E., and Kimberly, John R. 1984. "Paradox, Planning, and Perseverance: Guidelines for Managerial Practice." In *New Futures:*

References

The Challenge of Managing Corporate Transitions. Edited by John R. Kimberly and Robert E. Quinn. Homewood, IL: Dow Jones-Irwin.

Tichy, Noel M. 1983. *Managing Strategic Change: Technical, Political, and Cultural Dynamics.* New York: Wiley.

Chapter Notes

NOTES ON CHAPTER 1

1. The above account is taken from William J. Abernathy, Kim B. Clark, and Alan M. Kantrow, *Industrial Renaissance* (New York: Basic Books, 1983), pp. 32–33.

2. Daniel Bell, *Work and Its Discontents* (Boston: Beacon Press, 1956), p. 10.

3. Garry Emmons, "David Birch: Putting the Numbers to Work," *Harvard Business School Bulletin*, April 1984, p. 54.

4. Michael J. Piore and Charles F. Sabel, *The Second Industrial Divide* (New York: Basic Books, 1984), pp. 115–120.

5. Barbara Tuchman, "Mankind's Better Moments," *Wilson Quarterly*, Autumn 1980, p. 99.

6. Peter Pascarelli, "POWER: The World Series Ticket." *Inside Sports*, November 1983, pp. 42–48. One disclaimer here. Because of artificial turf (and certain cavernous ballparks), an emphasis on speed relative to power can work—as the St. Louis Cardinals have demonstrated

in recent years. On natural turf, however, power hitting will usually prevail.

7. The United States' distinctive experience with mass production is extensively documented in Piore and Sabel, *Industrial Divide*.

8. Frederick C. Klein, "Star Wars: Competition Across National Boundaries," *The Wall Street Journal*, January 4, 1983, p. 28.

9. Ken Dryden, *The Game* (New York: Times Books, 1983), pp. 222–236.

10. Conversation with Doug Wilson, *MBA*, May 29, 1987.

11. William H. Whyte, "The Organization Man: A Rejoinder," The Business World, *The New York Times Magazine*, December 7, 1986, p. 98.

12. David Birch, quoted by James Cook, "Bring on the Wild and Crazy People," *Forbes*, April 28, 1986, p. 56.

NOTES ON CHAPTER 2

1. Sociotechnical systems theory, first articulated by Eric Trist, does span these two worlds. (See E. L. Trist & K. W. Bamforth, "Some Social and Psychological Consequences of the Longwall Method of Coal-Getting," *Human Relations*, 4, 1951, pp. 3–38; and E. L. Trist, G. W. Higgin, H. Murray, & A. B. Pollock, *Organizational Choice* [London: Tavistock, 1963].) This perspective argues that optimal organizational performance depends on jointly optimizing the social and the technical aspects of work. However, applications of sociotechnical theory have largely been restricted to "micro" organizational units—to small groups and plants made up of such groups (i.e., to groups of groups). Common terms for such applications are "autonomous work-team" structures, "high-commitment/performance work systems," and "team concept." Calvin Pava has extended the sociotechnical approach to managerial levels, but the focal units are still micro (C. H. P. Pava, *Managing New Office Technology* [New York: Free Press, 1983]). The relation between sociotechnical systems applications and the concepts developed in this chapter is captured by the following enclosed shape:

SOCIOTECHNICAL SYSTEMS THEORY

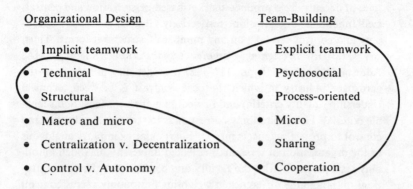

Organizational Design	Team-Building
• Implicit teamwork	• Explicit teamwork
• Technical	• Psychosocial
• Structural	• Process-oriented
• Macro and micro	• Micro
• Centralization v. Decentralization	• Sharing
• Control v. Autonomy	• Cooperation

2. Robert E. Levinson, *The Decentralized Company* (New York: AMACOM, 1983).

3. Edmund T. Pratt, Jr., quoted in *Wharton Alumni Magazine*, Fall 1986, p. 16.

4. James O'Toole, *Vanguard Management* (Garden City, NY: Doubleday, 1985), p. 321.

5. Notable exceptions are the contrasting "multidimensional" designs presented by William C. Goggin in "How the Multidimensional Structure Works at Dow Corning," *Harvard Business Review*, January–February 1974, pp. 54–65; and by Russell L. Ackoff in *Creating the Corporate Future* (New York: Wiley, 1981), pp. 153–163. In fact, much of the academic literature on organizational design/behavior/change is triadic. In a recent article, "Team Sports Models as a Generic Organizational Framework" (*Human Relations*, 40, September 1987, pp. 591–612). I identify several theoretical schemes that parallel the construct developed in this book. Why hasn't more of this literature penetrated popular management usage? My sense is that the specialized vocabularies typically used by academics are difficult for practitioners to grasp.

6. Stanley M. Davis, *Future Perfect*, (Reading, MA: Addison-Wesley, 1987), p. 83. In fact, this polar opposition also predominates in the political-economy literature. As Robert B. Reich has shown in *Tales of a New America* (New York: Times Books, 1987), issues continue to be framed narrowly as a contest between conservatism/free markets (autonomy) on the one hand and liberalism/governmental planning (control) on the other.

7. Autonomy and control typically match up with the standard alternatives of decentralized product/market-based organization and centralized functional organization, respectively. But as processes, autonomy and control can take on any number of structural forms. Thus, Jay Galbraith (*Designing Complex Organizations* [Reading, MA: Addison-Wesley, 1973], pp. 117–118) provides an example from the aerospace industry in which the core contrast is between technical leadership (quality criteria) and project management (cost and schedule criteria). Here, autonomy corresponds to technical leadership and control to project management. This particular example is analogous to the organization of a research-oriented university, in which autonomy rests primarily with the faculty and control with the administration—although the difference in weighting (autonomy versus control) reflects the difference between a convergent manufacturer and a divergent educational institution.

8. The unlikelihood of getting the best of three worlds has been recognized not only in corporate contexts but in social research and in theoretical mathematics. In social research, Warren Thorngate's postulate of commensurate complexity argues that no theory of social behavior can be simultaneously general, accurate, and simple. It can be any one or two of these things, but not all three (W. Thorngate, " 'In general' vs. 'it depends': Some Comments on the Gergen-Schlenker Debate," *Personality and Social Psychology Bulletin* 2, 1976, pp. 404–410). Karl Weick suggests that "much organizational research is uninformative and pedestrian partly because people have tried to make it general *and* accurate *and* simple. In trying to accommodate all three of these aims, none have been realized vigorously; the result has been bland assertions." (Karl E. Weick, *The Social Psychology of Organizing,* 2nd ed. [Reading, MA: Addison-Wesley, 1979], p. 41.) In mathematics, Kurt Gödel demonstrated through his incompleteness theorem that no theory of all mathematics is finitely describable, consistent, and complete (Rudy Rucker, *Mind Tools: The Five Levels of Mathematical Reality* [Boston: Houghton Mifflin, 1987], pp. 218–226).

9. George Lakoff and Mark Johnson, *Metaphors We Live By* (Chicago: University of Chicago, 1980).

10. The study was carried out by Josephine Olson, a business professor at the University of Pittsburgh. According to *The New York Times*, "The study discovered that among 1,200 [male] graduates of the school's M.B.A. program, individual income rose by an average of

$600 for every additional inch of height. Somebody 6-foot 2, for instance, collected a nice $6,000 more than someone 5-foot 4." (N. R. Kleinfield, "For Tall Executives: Two Bumps a Day, $600 an Inch," *The New York Times*, March 8, 1987, p. 6F.)

11. Bill Russell, *Second Wind* (New York: Random House, 1979), p. 83.

12. Richard Tanner Pascale and Anthony G. Athos, *The Art of Japanese Management* (New York: Simon & Schuster, 1981), p. 121.

13. Red Auerbach, quoted by Frank Deford, "A Man for All Seasons," *Sports Illustrated,* Feb. 15, 1982, p. 60.

14. Galbraith, *Designing Complex Organizations.*

15. Harold J. Leavitt, *Managerial Psychology*, 2nd ed. (Chicago: University of Chicago, 1972).

16. McKinsey & Company, Inc., New York: McKinsey Staff Paper, 1979.

17. Jay Galbraith, *Organization Design* (Reading, MA: Addison-Wesley, 1977).

18. *Van Nostrand's Scientific Encyclopedia*, 5th ed. (New York: Van Nostrand Reinhold, 1976), p. 615.

NOTES ON CHAPTER 3

1. Frederick Terman, quoted by Everett M. Rogers and Judith K. Larsen, *Silicon Valley Fever* (New York: Basic Books), 1984, p. 36.

2. Arno Penzias, quoted by Gene Bylinsky, "Can Bell Labs Keep It Up?" *Fortune*, June 27, 1983, p. 91.

3. Edward M. Scolnik, quoted in "Giving Free Rein to Merck's Best and Brightest," *Business Week*, October 19, 1987, p. 90.

4. Christopher Alexander, Murray Silverstein, Schlomo Angel, Sara Ishikawa, and Denny Abrams, *The Oregon Experiment* (New York: Oxford University, 1975), p. 48.

5. Ann Monroe, "Morgan Stanley Banks on a Hybrid Strategy as Its World Changes," *The Wall Street Journal*, June 27, 1985, pp. 1 & 22.

6. Gary Hector, "A Go-Go Insurer Adds Zest to Life," *Fortune*, March 5, 1984, p. 52.

7. Alfred Lohner, quoted by Richard Reeves, "Heartbreaker on Wheels," *The New York Times Magazine*, December 29, 1985, p. 21.

8. Marcelo A. Gumucio, quoted in "Where Three Sales a Year Make You a Superstar," *Business Week*, February 17, 1986, p. 77.

9. Donald Rose, quoted by Janet Guyon and Charles W. Stevens, "AT&T's Bell Labs Adjusts to Competitive Era," *The Wall Street Journal*, August 13, 1985, p. 6.

10. John Merwin, "McOil Change," *Forbes*, August 11, 1986, pp. 91–92.

11. Robert Bass, quoted by Patricia Bellew Gray, "Hyatt Legal Services' Fast Growth Leaves Trail of Management Woes," *The Wall Street Journal*, May 6, 1987, p. 33.

12. Howard Rudnitsky, "Art Williams and His Part-Time Army," *Forbes*, June 3, 1985, p. 105.

13. These issues are discussed at length in Ian Lustick, "Explaining the Variable Utility of Disjointed Incrementalism: Four Propositions," *The American Political Science Review*, June 1980, p. 348.

14. "Collaboration," Honeywell Control Systems General Managers' Meeting, Fall 1985.

15. Steve Lohr, "Making Cars the Volvo Way," *The New York Times*, June 23, 1987, pp. D1, D5. Although U.S. automakers have yet to reconfigure the assembly line so radically as Volvo has done, they have begun to apply the same principles to new-car design. "Simultaneous engineering" is one term used to describe the process of getting all the relevant functions/departments together at the start of a program, rather than involving them sequentially, as used to be the case.

16. Stephen Fox, *The Mirror Makers* (New York: Morrow, 1984), p. 253.

17. Russell L. Ackoff, *Management in Small Doses* (New York: Wiley, 1986), p. 24.

18. Bill McGowan, quoted in "Face-to-Face," *Inc.*, August 1986, p. 34.

19. John Corson, quoted by David Shribman, "University in Virginia Creates a Niche, Aims to Reach Top Ranks," *The Wall Street Journal*, September 30, 1985, p. 13.

20. Subrata N. Chakravarty and Ruth Simon, "Has the World Passed Kodak By?" *Forbes*, November 5, 1984, p. 190.

21. Russell L. Ackoff, Jamshid Gharajedaghi, and Elsa Vergara Finnel,

A Guide to Controlling Your Corporation's Future (New York: Wiley, 1984), p. 122.

22. Robert M. Price, quoted in "Now, R&D Is Corporate America's Answer to Japan Inc., " *Business Week*, June 23, 1986, p. 135.

23. "Daewoo vs. Hyundai: Battle of the Korean Giants," *Business Week*, December 15, 1986, pp. 72–73.

24. James D. Thompson, *Organizations in Action* (New York: McGraw-Hill, 1967), pp. 54–55.

25. Russell Shaw, "T. Marshall Hahn, Jr.," *Sky*, June 1985, pp. 62–70.

26. Phyllis Grann, quoted by N. R. Kleinfield, "A Golden Touch for Best Sellers," *The New York Times Magazine*, April 7, 1985, p. 60.

27. Donald K. Clifford, Jr. and Richard E. Cavanagh, *The Winning Performance* (New York: Bantam, 1985), p. 95.

28. Daniel Machalaba, "United Parcel Service Gets Deliveries Done by Driving Its Workers," *The Wall Street Journal*, April 22, 1986, pp. 1, 23.

29. "These Traders Made All-Star by Hitting Singles," *Business Week*, November 3, 1986, p. 127.

30. Harold Geneen, with Alvin Moscow, *Managing* (Garden City, NY: Doubleday, 1984), p. 94.

31. Lucien Rhodes, "The Un-manager," *Inc.*, August 1982, p. 44.

32. My use of coordinating mechanism and decision system parallels, respectively, Ackoff et al.'s use of "coordination" and "integration" Ackoff et al., *A Guide*, pp. 8–9.

33. "Management's Newest Star," *Business Week*, October 13, 1986, pp. 160–172.

34. Michael W. Miller, "In This Futuristic Office, Intimacy Exists between Workers Separated by 500 Miles," *The Wall Street Journal*, June 27, 1986, p. 29.

35. Ackoff, *Small Doses*, p. 69.

36. Anthony J. F. O'Reilly, quoted in "The New Economy Suits Heinz's Stingy C.E.O," *Fortune*, June 23, 1986, p. 22.

37. Edwin A. Finn, Jr., "General Eclectic," *Forbes*, March 23, 1987, p. 80.

38. Robert E. Mullane, quoted in "How to Outearn the Boss and Keep Your Job," *Fortune*, May 27, 1985, p. 73.

39. Alex Kotlowitz, "Caterpillar, UAW Are Said to Agree Tentatively on Pact with Wage Freeze," *The Wall Street Journal*, July 7, 1986, p. 5.

40. "Labor Letter," *The Wall Street Journal*, March 31, 1987, p. 1.

41. Ben Weberman, "Goldman's Gilt," *Forbes*, February 24, 1986, p. 96.

42. Kenneth Iverson, quoted by Steven Prokesch, "Remaking the American CEO," *The New York Times*, January 3, 1987, p. 8F.

43. John Merwin, "A Tale of Two Worlds," *Forbes*, June 16, 1986, pp. 101–106.

44. Herbert J. Gans, *The Levittowners* (New York: Pantheon, 1967), p. 157.

45. Thomas J. Peters and Robert H. Waterman, Jr., *In Search of Excellence* (New York: Harper & Row, 1982), p. 220.

46. Christopher Alexander, Sara Ishikawa, and Murray Silverstein, with Max Jacobson, Ingrid Fiksdahl-King, and Schlomo Angel, *A Pattern Language*. (New York: Oxford University, 1977), pp. 410–411.

47. Stanley M. Davis, *Managing Corporate Culture* (Cambridge, MA: Ballinger, 1984), p. 8.

48. Robert S. Greenberger and Monica Langley, "Col. North's Ideology and Zealousness Led Him to Contras' Cause," *The Wall Street Journal*, December 31, 1986, p. 1.

49. Lee Smith, "The Lures and Limits of Innovation," *Fortune*, October 20, 1980, p. 91.

50. Rod Zilles, quoted by Robert Levering, Milton Moskowitz, and Michael Katz, *The 100 Best Companies to Work for in America* (Reading, MA: Addison-Wesley, 1984), p. 246.

51. Cited in Curtis W. Tarr, "How to Humanize MBAs," *Fortune*, March 31, 1986, p. 153.

52. "Rebuilding to Survive," *Time*, February 16, 1987, p. 45.

53. Reprinted in Clifford and Cavanagh, *Winning Performance*, p. 181.

54. This quotation and the account that follows are taken from Monica Langley, "ITT Chief Emphasizes Harmony, Confidence and Playing by Rules," *The Wall Street Journal*, September 13, 1984, pp. 1, 23.

55. Mary Williams Walsh, "Company-Built Retreats Reflect Firms' Cul-

tures and Personalities," *The Wall Street Journal*, August 16, 1984, p. 27.

NOTES ON CHAPTER 4

1. Thus, according to James L. Heskett (*Managing in the Service Economy* [Boston: Harvard Business School Press, 1986], p. 77): "Today, banks, insurance companies, real estate brokers, and investment banks all define their businesses as financial services. None of the leading institutions in these industries can take the chance of defining their businesses more narrowly, but they are all on a collision course. Further, they are being joined by firms whose bases of interest are as diverse as retailing and travel-related services."

2. A third vulnerability, the relative absence of just one form of teamwork, cannot be captured by the graphic; this omission has not proved to be material in my use of the Teamwork Triangle.

3. See, for example, Richard Beckhard and Reuben T. Harris, *Organizational Transitions: Managing Complex Change* (Reading, MA: Addison-Wesley, 1977), pp. 76–84; and Joseph E. McCann and Thomas N. Gilmore, "Diagnosing Organizational Decision Making through Responsibility Charting," *Sloan Management Review*, Winter 1983, pp. 3–15.

4. Most of what has been written about responsibility charting recommends a four-word vocabulary; the distinction is usually made between (1) the responsibility (hence the label *responsibility* charting) for taking initiative, developing alternatives, and otherwise "staffing" a decision, and (2) the final authority for approving or signing off on the decision. With corporate teams at a variety of levels, however, I have found such a vocabulary cumbersome and confusing—perhaps because the responsibility for "staffing" a decision has rarely been separated from the authority for "making" it. After a number of mixed experiences, I simplified the vocabulary to three words. The abridged vocabulary lost little if anything in richness and has proven to be considerably more understandable and usable. In other cases (especially in staff-intensive organizations) where decision *staffing* and decision *making* tend to be more separate, a four-word vocabulary may be preferable.

5. A useful exposition on norms and a technique called the "norm census" can be found in Fritz Steele and Stephen Jenks, *The Feel of the Work Place* (Reading, MA: Addison-Wesley, 1977), pp. 41-80.

NOTES ON CHAPTER 5

1. Kenneth N. M. Dundas and Peter R. Richardson, "Implementing the Unrelated Product Strategy," *Strategic Management Journal*, Vol. 3, 1982, pp. 287-301; Michael E. Porter, "From Competitive Advantage to Corporate Strategy," *Harvard Business Review*, May–June 1987, pp. 43-59.

2. Clifford and Cavanagh, *Winning Performance*, p. 11.

3. Paul J. Schierl, remarks to The Finance Forum, University of Notre Dame, February 18, 1987.

4. Bob Swiggett, quoted by Clifford and Cavanagh, *Winning Performance*, p. 83.

5. John P. Stack, quoted by Lucien Rhodes, with Patricia Amend, "The Turn-around," *Inc.*, August 1986, p. 44.

6. "The Crisis That Endangers Phelps Dodge," *Business Week*, July 26, 1982, p. 58.

7. Edwin P. Land, quoted by H. Igor Ansoff, *Strategic Management* (New York: Macmillan, 1979), p. 125.

8. Al Davis, quoted by Dave Anderson, *The Story of Football* (New York: Morrow, 1985), p. 92.

9. John Wooden, *Practical Modern Basketball*, 2nd ed. (New York: Wiley, 1980), p. 14.

10. Jay R. Galbraith & Robert J. Kazanjian, *Strategy Implementation*, 2nd ed. (St. Paul, MN: West, 1986), pp. 50-67.

11. Richard N. Foster, *Innovation: The Attackers Advantage* (New York: Summit Books, 1986), p. 178.

12. Frances Gaither Tucker, Seymour M. Zivan, and Robert C. Camp, "How To Measure Yourself Against the Best," *Harvard Business Review*, January–February 1987, p. 9.

13. The relation between mission and organizational design is analogous to that between strategy and structure(/style). For years, debates have raged over which is more important, which is "prior" to the other. The sensible response, I believe, is that of Galbraith and Kazanjian (*Strategy Implementation*, p. 144): "Overall . . . consistency must exist between strategy and all elements of the structure. What is important is not whether structure causes strategy, or vice versa, but whether they are eventually brought into line. In many causal sequences, change of strategy may precede change of structure. Or performance may decline, precipitating first a strategy change and then a structure change. Or structure may be changed first to bring in new managers who will formulate the new strategy. There is no simple one-to-one relation such as structure follows strategy."

14. Henry Mintzberg, "Organization Design: Fashion or Fit?" *Harvard Business Review*, January–February 1981, p. 115.

15. Kenichi Ohmae, "Transform Leaden Strategies into Golden Opportunities," *The Wall Street Journal*, December 24, 1984, p. 6.

NOTES ON CHAPTER 6

1. Ackoff, Gharajedaghi, and Finnel, *Controlling Corporation's Future*, pp. 44–45.

2. Steven Bach, quoted by Karen Heller, "Lights, Camera! The Inside Scoop on 'Heaven's Gate,'" *USA Today*, July 31, 1985, p. 2D.

3. Charles Simonyi, quoted by Thomas J. Lueck, "Once a Prodigy, Xerox Faces Midlife Crisis," *The New York Times*, September 30, 1984, p. 8F.

4. Jim Swiggett, interviewed in "Face-to-Face," *Inc.*, February 1987, p. 35.

5. Richard E. Walton, "From Control to Commitment in the Workplace," *Harvard Business Review*, March–April 1985, pp. 76–84.

6. For a provocative discussion of organizational adaptation and adaptability in the context of loose coupling, see Karl E. Weick, "Management of Organizational Change Among Loosely Coupled Elements," in Paul S. Goodman and Associates, *Change in Organizations* (San Francisco: Jossey-Bass, 1982), pp. 386–391.

Chapter Notes

7. Bela Gold, "CAM Sets New Rules for Production," *Harvard Business Review*, November–December 1982, p. 89.

8. "Thinking Ahead Got Deere in Big Trouble," *Business Week*, December 8, 1986, p. 69.

9. Karen Tolland, quoted by Erik Larson and Carrie Dolan, "Large Computer Firms Sprout Little Divisions for Good, Fast Work," *The Wall Street Journal*, August 19, 1983, p. 17.

10. Karen Tolland, quoted in "Two Lessons in Failure from Silicon Valley," *Business Week*, September 10, 1984, pp. 78, 83.

11. "Growing Pains at People Express," *Business Week*, January 28, 1985, p. 91.

12. Susan Carey, "Lufthansa Jettisons Bureaucratic Baggage," *The Wall Street Journal*, September 30, 1986, p. 36.

13. My use of "stuck in the middle" parallels that of strategy theorist Michael Porter, who uses the expression to describe "a firm that engages in each generic strategy but fails to achieve any of them" (Michael E. Porter, *Competitive Advantage: Creating and Sustaining Superior Performance* [New York: Free Press, 1985], p. 16). Porter's three generic strategies are differentiation, cost leadership, and focus; these correspond respectively to my three bases for organizational design: autonomy, control, and cooperation.

14. The bulk of this example, including the quotations that follow, is taken from William Celis III, "Trammell Crow's Realignment Moves Stir Fears of Change in Partner Ranks," *The Wall Street Journal*, February 2, 1987, p. 7.

15. Stephen Phillips, "Why Trammell Crow's Star Salesman Is Persona Non Grata," *The New York Times*, March 22, 1987, p. 6F.

16. Foster, *Innovation: The Attacker's Advantage*, pp. 135, 151.

17. J. Richard Hackman, "The Transition That Hasn't Happened," in John R. Kimberly and Robert E. Quinn, *New Futures: The Challenge of Managing Corporate Transitions* (Homewood, IL: Dow Jones-Irwin, 1984), pp. 29–59. The following quotation is from p. 59.

18. This example and the quotations that follow are taken from "How Jim Treybig Whipped Tandem Back into Shape," *Business Week*, February 23, 1987, pp. 124–126.

19. *Ibid.*, p. 126.

20. *Ibid.*

21. Brian O'Reilly, "How Jimmy Treybig Turned Tough," *Fortune*, May 25, 1987, p. 104.

22. There may be as many definitions of "transformation" as there are writers (not to mention consultants) who use the word. Some representative meanings can be found in Amir Levy, "Second-Order Planned Change: Definition and Conceptualization," *Organizational Dynamics*, Summer 1986, pp. 4–23.

23. Harry A. Caunter, quoted in "McDonald's the Name, Fixing Gould Is the Game," *Business Week*, July 28, 1986, p. 77.

24. William T. Ylvisaker, quoted by Mark Potts and Peter Behr, *The Leading Edge* (New York: McGraw-Hill, 1987), pp. 74, 75.

25. "A New President to Fit Gould's New Shape," *Business Week*, July 30, 1984, pp. 78–79.

26. "McDonald's the Name," p. 77.

27. Harry A. Caunter, quoted by Alex Kotlowitz, "Gould's Ylvisaker Retires as Chairman; McDonald Is Seen as Likely Successor," *The Wall Street Journal*, September 3, 1986, p. 2.

NOTES ON CHAPTER 7

1. Paul Watzlawick, John H. Weakland, and Richard Fisch, *Change: Principles of Problem Formation and Problem Resolution* (New York: Norton, 1974), p. 19.

2. P. G. Herbst, *Socio-Technical Design: Strategies in Multidisciplinary Research* (London: Tavistock, 1974), pp. 19–27.

3. Gareth Morgan, *Images of Organization* (Beverly Hills: Sage Publications, 1986), pp. 106–107.

4. Christopher Alexander, *The Timeless Way of Building* (New York: Oxford University, 1979), p. 370.

5. Bill Marriott, quoted by Mike Sheridan, "J. W. Marriott, Jr.," *Sky*, March 1987, p. 46.

6. Edson W. Spencer, quoted in "Conversation with Edson W. Spencer and Fosten A. Boyle," *Organizational Dynamics*, Spring 1983, p. 43.

7. Meredith Belbin, *Management Teams* (New York: Wiley, 1981), p. 56.

8. Peter Drucker, cited in "Management's Biggest Mistakes," *Small Business Report*, December 1986, p. 59.

9. Fritz Steele, "The Ecology of Executive Teams: A New View of the Top," *Organizational Dynamics*, Spring 1983, pp. 65–78.

10. Edwin A. Finn, Jr., and Jack Willoughby, "Teaching Old Banks New Tricks," *Forbes*, June 15, 1987, p. 36.

11. Belbin, *Management Teams*, p. 130.

12. Reginald Jones, Advanced Management Program, Harvard Business School, April 15, 1982; cited by Charles Fombrun, Noel M. Tichy, and Mary Anne Devanna, *Strategic Human Resource Management* (New York: Wiley, 1984), p. 199.

13. Michael Brody, "NASA's Challenge: Ending Isolation at the Top," *Fortune*, May 12, 1986, p. 26.

14. The Disney and Delta examples are taken from Heskett, *Managing in the Service Economy*, pp. 58, 127.

15. Zane E. Barnes, "Change in the Bell System," *Academy of Management Executive*, February 1987, p. 45.

16. Ken Iverson, quoted in "Face-to-Face," *Inc.*, April 1986, p. 44.

17. James J. Renier, "Turnaround of Information Systems at Honeywell," *Academy of Management Executive*, February 1987, p. 50.

18. The question of appropriate organizational integration is a key to successful corporate mergers and acquisitions—even if this matter routinely receives only a fraction of the attention that it deserves. Indeed, there is evidence that people matches are more important than financials to long-term organizational effectiveness ("Labor Letter," *The Wall Street Journal*, August 26, 1986, p. 1).

    From an organizational design standpoint, assessing potential corporate combinations is no different from diagnosing the existing organization. There are three ideal types of combinations, which correspond to the vertices of the Teamwork Triangle. In an autonomy arrangement, the two organizations remain separate; in a control arrangement, one becomes subordinate to (a subset of) the other; and with cooperation, the two organizations form an undifferentiated whole.

    Realistically, every merger/acquisition represents a blend of these three types. What is critical is that both parties understand the nature of their particular blend and are committed to making it work. The Teamwork Profile can help them test the degree of mutual understanding and acceptance.

19. Heskett, *Managing in the Service Economy*, p. 17.

20. This line of approach is developed at length in Paul R. Lawrence and Jay W. Lorsch's classic, *Organization and Environment: Managing Differentiation and Integration* (Boston: Harvard University, 1967), and in Galbraith's *Designing Complex Organizations*.

21. Rensis Likert, *The Human Organization: Its Management and Value* (New York: McGraw-Hill, 1967), pp. 51–52.

22. Ackoff, Gharajedaghi, and Finnel, *Controlling Your Corporation's Future*, pp. 15–16, 18.

23. Unpublished notes of Edward Boehm, quoted by Philip Selznick, *Leadership in Administration* (New York: Harper & Row, 1957), pp. 53–54.

24. Foster, *Innovation: The Attacker's Advantage*, p. 210. The same advice holds for firms whose parts represent different centers of gravity—that is, different stages along the raw materials (upstream)-to-consumer (downstream) sequence. According to Galbraith and Kazanjian, a company can manage units with different centers of gravity only if the latter are "separated and run as separate subsidiaries . . . . However, if the firm attempts to run equally dominant stages in an integrated fashion, difficulties will emerge" (*Strategy Implementation: Structure, Systems and Process*, p. 69).

25. Larry E. Greiner's five organizational growth stages ("Evolution and Revolution as Organizations Grow," *Harvard Business Review*, July–August 1972, pp. 37–46) match the organizational design dimensions as follows: creativity (autonomy), direction (control), delegation (autonomy), coordination (control), collaboration (cooperation). The teamwork methodology is also useful for tracking phases of new-product development. (See Robert W. Keidel, "Baseball, Football, and Basketball: Models for Business," *Organizational Dynamics*, Winter 1984, p. 11; and Robert W. Keidel and Michael J. Umen, "Winning Plays in the R&D Game," *Pharmaceutical Executive*, February 1984, pp. 42–44.)

I have found a simple, three-step method useful for mapping the trajectory of engineering/construction projects. First, the overall project is partitioned into phases. Second, the nature of the "game" represented by each phase is established (baseball/autonomy, football/control, basketball/cooperation, or a two-way hybrid). Third, the coach/manager and players (primary and supporting) are identified for each phase. If more detail is desired, this method can be followed up with systematic (phase-based) decision analysis, as described in Chapter 4.

NOTES ON CHAPTER 8

1. Gary Jobson, interviewed by Ted Koppel on *ABC News Nightline*, January 14, 1987.

2. Christopher Alexander, *The Timeless Way of Building* (New York: Oxford University, 1979), pp. 145–146.

3. Charles Osgood, *CBS Sunday Night News with Charles Osgood*, January 11, 1987.

4. Roger von Oech, *A Kick in the Seat of the Pants* (New York: Harper & Row, 1986), p. 44.

5. The following account is based on interviews with Abe Raab and Derek Wendelken, Plano, TX, March 8–9, 1987.

6. George M. Prince, *The Practice of Creativity* (New York: Collier Books, 1970).

7. Charlie Feld, quoted in "Frito-Lay, Inc.: A Strategic Transition," Harvard Business School Case 0-187-065, pp. 6–7.

8. Organizations have properties that resemble the mathematical concept of "fractal." According to Rudy Rucker (*Mind Tools: The Five Levels of Mathematical Reality*, p. 177): "... a shape is 'fractal' if it has similar-looking structures on several different size scales—a line that branches into lines that branch into lines that branch; a bump covered with bumps that are covered with bumps that are bumpy; a glob made of globs made of globs of globs. ... Fractals ... have *more* detail than expected. Typically, examining a fractal twice as closely will give you more than twice as much information." By analogy, the deeper one takes the Teamwork Profile into an organization, the more information that will be elicited.

9. Morgan, *Images of Organization*, p. 97.

10. "Emerson Electric: High Profits from Low Tech," *Business Week*, April 4, 1983, p. 62.

11. Michael E. Porter, *Competitive Advantage: Creating and Sustaining Superior Performance*, pp. 414–415. This hybrid parallels a number of other organizational constructs, including Emery and Trist's combination of "social pluralism" and "unifying ground" (F. E. Emery and E. L. Trist, *Towards a Social Ecology: Contextual Appreciations of the Future in the Present* [London: Plenum, 1973]); Miles and Snow's "market-matrix organization" (Raymond E. Miles and Charles C. Snow, *Organizational Strategy, Structure, and Process* [New York: McGraw-Hill, 1978]); and McCaskey's combination of "network" and "core group" (Michael B. McCaskey, *The Executive Challenge: Managing Change and Ambiguity* [Marshfield, MA: Pitman, 1982]).

12. This statement and the material that follows are taken from *Saab 1987* and *Saab 1988* (brochures). (Orange, CT: Saab-Scania of America), 1986, 1987.

13. Ramchandran Jaikumar, "Postindustrial Manufacturing," *Harvard Business Review*, November–December 1986, p. 76.

14. Weick, *Psychology of Organizing*, p. 133.

15. Steven I. Schlossberg, quoted by John Hoerr, "America's Labor Laws Weren't Written for a Global Economy," *Business Week*, January 13, 1986, p. 38.

16. George A. Keyworth II, quoted in "Passing the Buck in R&D Financing," *Business Week*, December 2, 1985, p. 34.

17. William J. Baumol, "A Modest Decline Isn't All That Bad," *The New York Times*, February 15, 1987, p. 2-F. In fact, enlightened appreciations of sport also transcend zero-sum thinking. Thus, according to former Olympic decathlon champion Bill Toomey, "In the old days, the Russians took pictures of us in track and field. Then all of a sudden we were filming [high jumper] Valery Brumel. That's the way it works. You share with each other because competition is the name of the game. Tables will always turn, but in the long run it makes us all better." (quoted in "Newly at a Loss for Worlds," *Time*, September 28, 1987, p. 43).

Author Index

Author Index

Author Index

Subject
Index

Subject Index

Automatic Data Processing, Inc. (ADP), 106, 200
Automobile industry
  joint ventures and, 50
  player autonomy and, 38–39
  voluntary cooperation and, 46–47
Autonomy. *See also* Autonomy-based organization
  age of, 2
  automobile industry and, 38–39
  decentralization and, 17
  educational, 10–11
  family and, 201–202
  manager-controller versus, 44–45
  organizational design and, 31
  relative importance of, by era, 14
  society and, 202
  specifying norms and, 100
  as strategic problem in redesigning organization, 125–128
  structural forms and, 216
  too much, 125–128
Autonomy-based organization, 37–41. *See also* Autonomy
  architect role in, 156
  collaborator role in, 156
  products of, 39–41
Autonomy/control hybrid, 193
  effective, 194
Autonomy/cooperation hybrid, 192–193
  conceptualization of, 197
  delicate balance in, 200
  independence and interdependence in, 199–200
  matrix as bridge to, 194
  as new organization form, 195
  organizational features of, 197

Back-and-forth coordinating mechanism, 53–54
Bally Manufacturing, 63
Baltimore Orioles, 112
Bank of America, 72
Baseball as model, 7–8, 9
  decentralized organization and, 24–25

vertical organizational design and, 25
Basketball as model, 7, 8
L.L. Bean, 116
Bell Communications Research, Inc. (Bellcore), 50
Bell Labs, 38, 41
Belonging, sense of, 72–73
Bernbach, W., 47, 112
Bias, cultural. *See* Cultural bias
Bonus formula, 66
Boston Celtics, 25, 27, 112
Brainstorming, 124
Broad-form insurance policies, 161
Brother Industries, Ltd., 118
Bureaucracy
  consensus degenerated into, 130
  functional, 3–4
Business, world society and, 205–206
Business administration graduate, height and earnings of, 24
Business Week, 40, 113, 128, 143, 150, 151, 195
Business-as-a-game philosophy, 111–112
Buyers, organizational strategy and, 48–49

Capabilities
  mission component and, 107–109
  unit or functional, corporate capabilities and, 176–177
Caterpillar, 49, 110
Centralization
  decision making and, 56–57
  football and, 25
  organizational assessment and, 91
  organizational design and, 17, 26
  prototype of, 26
  reduction of, 147
Centrifugal tendencies, 127
Change, 132–152
  adjustment in, 133–137
  commitment to, 154
  doglegged, 149
  implementation of, 153–181

Subject Index

Freedom, organizational design and, 17
Free-standing roles/units, 51–52
Frito-Lay, Inc., 110, 188–190
Frontier Airlines, 139, 140, 141
Functional bureaucracy, 3–4
Functional capabilities biased towards corporate capabilities, 176–177

Gar Wood, 179
General Electric, 63, 113, 167, 200
General Motors, 4, 45, 66, 89, 112, 171
General Schedule, civil service, 64
Geography of customer, 106
George Mason University, 49
Georgia-Pacific, 52
Glasnost, 203
Global coordination, control and, 41–45, 46, 59–60
Goal acceptance, 22
Goldman Sachs, 66
Golf, 149
W. L. Gore & Associates, 59, 195
Gore-tex, 58
Gould Inc., 149–151
G. P. Putnam's Sons, 54
Graduate business schools, teamwork and, 10
Graphic displays, 165–166
Graphics, inter-unit complementarity and, 75
Green Bay Packers, 109, 112
Greyhound Corporation, 78
Group assessment, subjectivity in, 89–102
Groups meetings, team integration and, 174
Growth
  joint ventures and, 50
  organizational, 227–228
  organizational strategy and, 48–50

Hartmann, 109
Harvard Business Review, 116
Heinz Co., 62

Herman Miller, 72
Hewlett-Packard, 53–54, 57, 74, 155, 195
Hierarchic organization, 52–53
  control-orientation and, 42
  mutualistic approaches and, 66
  reward system and, 63–65
Hierarchical levels, reduction of, 197
Hierarchical planning, 52–53
  control-orientation and, 42
High-volume manufacturing
  control-based organization and, 42, 43
  mandating and, 56
  programmed interaction and, 68
Hillerich & Bradsby, 41
Historical referents, 113
History of teamwork. *See* Teamwork, history of
H. J. Heinz Co., 62
Holding company, 26
Holiday Inns, 110
Hologram, organization conceptualized as, 191–192
Honda of America, 66, 67
Honeywell, 46, 75, 110, 163, 172
Horizontal organizational design
  basketball and, 25
  team-building and, 24
Horizontal work/information flow, vertical authority patterns and, 58
Hyatt Legal Services, 43
Hyundai, 50

IBM, 72, 155
Ice hockey, teamwork in, 9
Idealized system redesign, 122
Implicit teamwork through organizational design, 16–21
Inc., 111
Independent action, 68. *See also* Autonomy
  autonomy/cooperation hybrid and, 199–200
Individual expectation, 71–73
  assessment and, 92–93, 101

Subject Index

Pacific Telesis Group (PacTel), 66
Palo Alto Research Center (PARC), 127
Parallel coordinating mechanism, 51–52
Participative management
  need for increase in, 145
  organizational design and team-building and, 28
  transformation and, 151
  transition from, 141–142
People Express Airlines, 72, 130, 139, 140, 141
PepsiCo, Inc., 189, 200
Perception of organization, sampling of, 89–90
Performance level, 111–116
Performance referents
  external, 112, 114–116
  internal, 112, 113–114
  time orientation of, 112–113
  types of, 112
Permutation, 161–162
Personal computer (PC), 58
Pfizer, Inc., 17
Phelps Dodge Corp., 113
Physical configuration
  assessment of, 92
  cooperation and, 159, 171–172
  effect of, 67–69
  separateness and, 68
Planning, hierarchical, 52–53
Player autonomy, 44–45
  automobile industry and, 38–39
Player identification in control-based organization, 44
Polaroid, 114
Pooled interdependence, 51–54
Porsche, 39, 46
Postindustrial era, 4–7
Preindustrial era, 2
Princeton University, 49
Priorities, reweighting of, 137
Problem-solving/action-planning, 22
Procter & Gamble, 200
Product
  of autonomy-based organizations, 38–41

  market for, 90–91, 107
  obsolescence of, 150
Production/function matrix, 146
Product/market coherence, 107
Product/market growth, 90–91
Profit center, discrete, 52
Program control, administrative control and, 136–137
Programmed interaction, 68
Project teams, 5–6
Promotional practices, 90–91
Psychographics of customer, 107

Quality circles, 27, 133
Quality-of-work-life initiatives, 133–135
Quantitative measures of performance, 111

Raychem Corporation, 69
R&D multiplier, 115
Reality, names and, 154
Reciprocal interdependence, 51–54
Recommending course of action, 174
Recruitment/promotional practices, 90–91
Redesigning of organization, 121–152
  change routes in, 132–152
    adustment and, 133–137
    transformation and, 149–152
    transition and, 137–149
  strategic problems of, 125–132
    absence of priorities in, 131–132
    too much autonomy in, 125–128
    too much control in, 128–129
    too much cooperation in, 129–131
  two-phase process of, 123–125
Reducing costs, 41–45
Reducing subjectivity, 89–102
Reference group in mission articulation, 111–116
Reification of names, 154
Resources
  for change, commitment of, 157
  internal, 49–50

Subject Index